KILLING WEAKNESS:

The Samurai's Path to Self-Actualization

Use This Warrior Method to Develop
Inner Strength and Find Your True Path

RYAN PEREZ

Disclaimer:
This book is not intended as a substitute for the medical advice of physicians or mental health professionals. The reader should consult a medical professional in matters relating to his/her health or mental health.

Samurai Reader
901 Ponce De Leon Blvd., Ste 101
Coral Gables, FL 33134-3059
Samuraireader.com
Contact the author: Ryan@samuraireader.com

Get the samurai reader starter library for free. Go to the Get Three Free eBooks section of this book to learn more.

ISBN paperback: 979-8-6899474-0-2

CONTENTS

Introduction

My mother died in the small bedroom of a run-down house that she shared with three other people, when she was just fifty-eight years old. She died broken and alone, prey to demons of her own making.

Drugs and alcohol were the official cause of her death, but in truth she had given up living long before she died. My mother was a mental prisoner, a slave to circumstance, tightly chained to her past and unable to escape the carnival of thoughts in her head.

She was a beautiful woman, but her physical beauty was merely a façade, a shell, that served only to hide the brokenness within.

My mother was unable to look at her actions objectively. Nothing was ever her fault; no action was ever egregious enough for her to accept responsibility for its outcome. Whether she was hiding empty bottles of vodka in my backpack when I was in elementary school or getting arrested for driving my infant brother around when she was blackout drunk. Nothing ever made her stand up, take note and say, this is my fault, I created this situation with my actions, and the only way I can fix it is by exercising my agency.

This blindness was, no doubt, the consequence of her upbringing. Her whole life she had been coddled by my grandparents. She was the youngest of three children and the only girl in an immigrant family. In seeking to protect her, my grandparents created a fundamental disconnect from reality, which made my mother incapable of seeing the correlation between actions and outcomes. Especially and most importantly, the correlation between her actions and negative outcomes.

Life, however, doesn't operate on our terms, and that blindness crippled her. When she was inevitably handed defeat, as we all are, she was unable to cope and turned to alcohol to heal what hurt. Rather than profit from her pain and learn the lesson that adversity had to teach, she chose to turn a deaf ear and a blind eye. Looking at reality, in all of its naked glory, was just too painful for her to bear.

This disconnect made the obstacles of her own making insurmountable. Her inability to gain momentum in life only caused her more pain, which in turn made it even harder for her to objectively analyze her actions, a vicious cycle that would continue for the rest of her life.

Growth is always painful. Whether it is physically when we are young or emotionally as we age, growth hurts. This pain means we are alive and evolving as human beings. It is the by-product of a correct perspective and an active life. Rather than embrace this pain and learn from it, she ran from it.

In seeking to escape the unpleasant aspects of her reality, my mother destroyed everything in her life and alienated every single person that loved her. Which, of course, only caused her more distress. She had three failed marriages, two estranged sons (from different fathers), and was incapable of maintaining steady employment, finding real friends, or having deep relationships with anyone. Each small bump on the road of life only added to the sum total of her pain. With no mechanism by which to heal and learn, she saw herself as the perpetual victim to malicious circumstances.

Taking ownership of the circumstances we find ourselves in and believing that their outcome is our fault (good or bad) is power. It means that we have agency to effect change. When we believe ourselves to be at the mercy of circumstance, we are powerless. This feeling of powerlessness creates a vacuum in our soul.

My mother chose to fill this vacuum with booze and pills. She chose not to fight, not to field an army against the forces of life. She let her demons conquer her inner citadel without resistance.

Unfortunately, my mother's story is not unique. According to the World Health Organization (WHO), 450 million people in the developed world suffer from a mental health disorder—depression and anxiety being chief among them. WHO claims that one in four people will be affected by mental or neurological disorders at some point in their lives.

But why? Even in the midst of a global pandemic, we, as a species, have never been more prosperous, interconnected, and safe than we are today. Yet despite this safety and comfort, we aren't happy. Reality simultaneously bores us and overwhelms us. We are, on average, fat, sad, and devoid of purpose. The former likely a result of the latter.

We aren't happy because safety and comfort are antithetical to the personal evolution that leads to self-actualization, which is the only source of lasting satisfaction. Our lives lack the basic struggles that were commonplace in generations past. We have strived to eliminate strife and continue to succeed.

Without strife and bereft of purpose, our mind turns the need for struggle inward. An unending carnival of thoughts consumes us, and unexamined patterns of behavior become us. Yet somewhere in the recess of our mind, we cling foolishly to hope. But we don't act on it—instead, we expect things to get better without any organized effort to this end. As if it is a natural consequence of existence that our lives should improve by virtue of simply being alive.

When reality fails to meet our unrealistic expectations, we become disheartened and lose faith in our agency without ever having really put it to the test. This leads to feelings of powerlessness. We believe ourselves to be at the mercy of circumstance and our mental state to be a matter of luck rather than a product of our efforts.

We see others who are masters of agency, bending reality to their will, and we invent reasons (meaning excuses) why we are not in their position (and with this perspective never will be). We grow resentful, sarcastic, pessimistic, and passive aggressive. We lose ourselves with each passing year, drifting further away from the person we once hoped we would become. Death finds us suddenly because we never really began living. We die afraid, resentful of how little time we had and how foolishly we spent the time we were given.

This crisis of purpose is a unique modern affliction. Previous generations were defined by strife and driven by purpose. They fought world wars, lived through rampant poverty, and fought for civil liberties (and that is only recent history). The further we delve into the past, the more dire mankind's situation becomes. The grit of the ancients is unimaginable to us today.

They acquired this mettle through exposure to extreme conflict—in other words, fighting wars of various kinds, overseas, at home, and in the workplace. War puts things into perspective. When consequences are dire and time is in short supply, priorities become clear and the superfluous falls away. What really matters is brought to the surface.

War, however, is not synonymous with violence. War is simply the highest form of struggle. It's a contest with a critical outcome. A game where all the chips are on the table and all the marbles are on the line. As Yagyū Munenori, the samurai philosopher, once wrote to the warriors in his command, "It is missing the point to think that the martial art is solely in cutting a man down. It is not in cutting people down; it is in killing evil."

Evil comes in many forms, among them the distraction, noise, and weakness that keeps us from becoming our higher selves. If war is a contest with a critical outcome, then what could be more of a war than our life? What necessitates more thought, preparation, attention, energy, and strife?

We battle different enemies in different seasons of our lives (ignorance, fear, mediocrity, hubris, and atrophy), but we are always on the field of battle till we breathe our last, and that too is a battle, to die with dignity, devoid of fear.

To deny that we are at war is to not field an army against the forces of life. It is akin to surrendering everything we love to the barbarian hordes. Failing to field our army leads to ennui, a feeling of listlessness that is dark, directionless, and devoid of purpose.

I know this feeling well. It's what I felt for most of my adult life. I was lost in the wilderness of my mind for a long, long time. Plagued by hereditary weakness, paralyzed by inertia, blinded by ego, consumed by hollow desires, and unable to generate any traction toward purpose. This was my reality for longer than I care to remember.

Then something changed. At the behest of a friend, I stumbled into a Brazilian Jujitsu class. At first, I was worse than terrible. I had smoked cigarettes for years and barely had the stamina to make it through a five-minute round of sparring, what is commonly referred to as "rolling" in Brazilian Jujitsu. The idea of defeating anyone was a far-fetched fantasy. Merely surviving a five-minute round felt like a monumental victory.

This forced confrontation with my own weakness left me with two choices, quit or improve. For perhaps the first time in my life I chose the hard road. Admittedly my overinflated ego was the key driving factor in this decision. I could not stomach the image of myself as a weakling, physically incapable of combat.

So I kept going back, and, as is common among new practitioners, I began to notice a change in myself, subtle and barely perceptible at first, then drastic and sudden. Unbeknownst to me, what was happening was the personal evolution that accompanies the pursuit of excellence in any arena.

Practicing martial arts is a vehicle for self-transcendence. We discover ourselves as we sharpen our skills and ultimately learn to leave the self behind as we ascend to ever-higher levels of proficiency. In the beginning I couldn't articulate this, but I could feel it. Every time I stepped on the tatami mat, I felt free and alive, and every time I stepped off, I felt a sense of accomplishment and improvement.

This was the exact opposite of what life was like outside of the gym. My journey into martial arts coincided with a tumultuous time in my life, both professionally and personally. I desperately wanted the same combination of purpose and peace of mind that I had on the mats in my everyday life.

As a natural extension of that desire and curiosity I began to study the roots of the art I was practicing, and I discovered a rich history—generations of warriors who often faced seemingly impossible odds and bleak circumstances with resolute conviction and a stout heart.

I was mesmerized by their seemingly superhuman strength of will. I not only read stories of their escapades but studied the principles that drove their actions and formed their world view.

It became abundantly clear to me that if I wanted that same strength of character and clarity of purpose, I, too, must live by the principles of martial philosophy. So I made a list of aphorisms (cited throughout this book) to use as guiding principles as I defined my purpose and began to execute my mission. This list became my manual, a road map for me to navigate difficult landscapes, both professionally and personally.

Executing my newly defined mission required me to free my mind from the heavy shackles grounding my ascent. The end of a long romantic relationship, my mother's untimely death, insecurities, fears of inadequacy, and a severe lack of capital, connections, and resources were all noise-emanating obstacles blocking the stillness needed to make objective observations and take effective action.

By absorbing the principles of martial philosophy and applying their lessons uniquely to my life, I was able not only to overcome the aforementioned barriers but turn them into the fuel needed to execute my mission with expediency. It is my hope that this writing will have a similar impact on your life. For this to come to fruition, however, requires not only absorption but a unique and diligent application of these principles to everyday existence.

The wisdom collected here is not my own. I've merely gathered the timeless insights of warriors from generations past and organized them in a way that was applicable to my life. Nor have I mastered these teachings. I've just found my path and have but begun walking it. I'm not enlightened. I'm not a guru, life coach, yogi, or healer, and I am prone to all kinds of errors and folly. Yet it is my hope that by walking my path I may serve as a guide to others seeking to find theirs.

This book is not an exercise in futility. It is not chock-full of catchy sayings meant to paint a pretty picture of existence. It is a road map for a systematic application of philosophical principles to daily life that changed the way I view and live my life in very real and tangible ways. This is my recipe for a meaningful and joyful existence. This approach, the acquisition of the warrior's spirit, will not work for everyone, but it did work for me.

ENTER THE SAMURAI

The warrior spirit reached the apex of its cultivation in feudal Japan. The island was dominated by warlords for hundreds of years. Whole provinces and entire clans were perpetually at war for centuries, and yet, despite this volatility, or perhaps because of it, life didn't only carry on, it flourished. Complex and culturally rich systems of order emerged, and a disciplined system of conduct was developed that elevated regular men to the heights of heroic warriors. These men were called samurai.

The samurai were a warrior class that rose from the lowest ranks to occupy the highest echelons of society. Yet they stood for more than mindless violence. Samurai were poets, artists, and administrators who were tasked with the governance and protection of their communities. They were beacons of strength, pillars of tranquility in a turbulent world, devoid of fear and indifferent to death.

If we are fated to fight life's many battles, then we should seek to acquire the spirit of the warrior and in doing so fortify our mind against the tyranny of circumstance. If we seek to acquire the spirit of the warrior, there exists no better blueprint to follow than one that, for more than a millennium, created some of the most formidable and fearless warriors the world has ever known. That blueprint is Bushido, the samurai's code of conduct that guided the warrior in both life and death.

There is no central Bushido text, like the Buddhist Pali Canon. Instead, individual samurai seeking to transmit the warrior spirit to later generations of their clansmen recorded for posterity not only their heroic deeds but also the philosophic principles governing their conduct.

By absorbing this philosophy and applying its lessons to our life, we too can free ourselves from the shackles of fear. Free from fear, with our perception cleansed, we can define and articulate our real aspirations, take action to fulfill them, and in doing so cultivate the best version of ourselves. So how do we gain the courage to face life like a samurai?

1

PRIME THE MIND

"Therefore those who would peacefully govern the land, the nation, and the home must first cultivate themselves."

—Naganuma Muneyoshi

In order to succeed in any arena, we first must recognize that the most pressing task at hand is the cultivation of our own mind. We cannot hope to govern a family, a company, or a nation if we cannot first govern ourselves.

The mind is both our compass and our canvas, a malleable tool we use to navigate life's many arenas. Our goal is to turn that tool into a weapon, to take our mind, once a blunt instrument, and turn it into a sharp edge. Then use that sharp edge to cut through the obstacles standing between us and the best version of ourselves.

In order for us to complete this transformative mission, we must live with intention. This means not floating passively from one moment to the next but rather asking ourselves, in every situation, who we want to be and how our ideal self would deal with the circumstance at hand, then electing how we want to act rather than reacting instinctively.

I learned how to elect behavior on the tatami mat by mimicking the master. I would watch my jujitsu professor spar with a blank, stoic expression on his face, deep in concentration, following his distinct pattern of rhythm, brief moments of stillness followed by smoothly calculated movements. This was light-years ahead of my jerky, sometimes explosive, mostly inefficient style of combat.

I also wore my emotions on my sleeve (or face, better said). When something hurt, I'd grimace; when tired, I'd breathe heavily and slow my movements. I was far from rhythmic or mysterious. I was easy to read and easy to beat.

To remedy this, I mimicked my professor. First in rhythm and later in demeanor. In the middle of a roll, I'd slow down and ask myself what my professor would do in this particular position. As I gave myself room to think, over time, explosive, jerky movements became timed attacks. As I learned to live with the discomfort of a disadvantageous position and push through it rather than immediately tapping, my easily perceptible emotions became an indecipherable poker face.

A lot of jujitsu involves ignoring our physical instincts. Incrementally working our way out of a bad, painful position when we want to quit, not panicking when someone grabs our neck or takes our back, rolling toward our opponent instead of away from them when they have us in a fully extended arm bar.

Jujitsu, like life, requires us to take control. I don't mean control of circumstances, as that would be impossible, but rather control of ourselves and how we react to circumstances, especially adverse circumstances. It seems obvious, but how many of us are really in control? Most of us are prisoners to our animal instincts, our lower selves.

2

OVERCOMING OUR INSTINCTS

BRAIN VERSUS MIND

The human brain, the soft, squishy, three-pound organ inside of our skull, is the most advanced organic computational instrument this world has ever produced. Through it we are able to peer into the inner workings of the universe and in doing so have come to understand our true origin.

The human brain is an organ of amazing complexity, four times larger than that of our closest primate cousin (chimpanzees), and though smaller in size than that of the minke whale (the largest mammalian brain on record), it has more neurons. About 74 billion more, to be exact. There are more neurons in the human brain than galaxies in the observable universe, and there are more interconnections among those neurons than there are stars in the Milky Way.

On an evolutionary scale the human brain evolved rather suddenly. Our brains tripled in size over the course of two million years. The factors fueling this relatively rapid evolution are believed to be these:

Infant Brain Development: The size of the human brain at the time of birth is limited by the pelvic girdle (size) of the mother. Simply put, women can't deliver large-headed babies. To contend with this challenge, humans (unlike other mammals) have evolved to extend the period of infant brain growth. Human infants' brains continue to grow for months after they are born.

Fire: Our abnormally large brains require an abnormal amount of energy. Science writer Jerry Adler described this evolutionary consequence succinctly: "The unprecedented increase in brain size that hominids embarked on around 1.8 million years ago had to be paid for with added calories either taken in or diverted from some other function in the body."

Fire and cooking are believed to be the instrument and method that solved this problem. "In essence, cooking—including not only heat but also mechanical processes such as chopping and grinding—outsources some of the body's work of digestion so that more energy is extracted from food and less expended in processing it. Cooking breaks down collagen, the connective tissue in meat, and softens the cell walls of plants to release their stores of starch and fat," according to Adler.

Cooking not only allowed humans to process food more efficiently and meet the caloric demands of our large brains but freed up time for other pursuits, including hunting, which demanded cooperation. The cooperation demanded by hunting (and the toolmaking necessary to hunt) may have been the catalyst for language, which in turn gave us our ability to cooperate socially, and social cooperation likely fueled the next leap forward in the evolution of the human brain. Language, then, was the critical prerequisite to social cooperation.

Language: Cognitive neuroscientists believe our brains are well wired for language. That is because the same neural region that we use for nonlinguistic behavior like manipulating objects and predicting sequences is the same neural region we use for linguistic behavior.

Anthropologist Dietrich Stout and neuroscientist Thierry Chaminade explain this overlap:

> Although language processing was long viewed as a functionally specialized and anatomically discrete module within the brain, it is now clear that the so-called "language areas" contribute to a wide array of nonlinguistic behaviors including tool use....This social thread was also picked up by subsequent workers, who considered the possible role of language in the transmission and coordination of early technologies, and suggested similarities between the sharing of arbitrary design concepts in the production of formal tool "types"

and the sharing of arbitrary symbolic associations in linguistic semantics.

In other words, language comes from and evolved with our necessity and capacity to make tools. Our words reflect the way we order our thoughts and our thoughts reflect the demands of our environment and our solutions to those demands. As solutions to those demands became more complex, the ability to communicate, organize, and cooperate became necessary.

Cooperation: Cooperation among early humans was necessary for survival. Complex behaviors such as hunting, cooking, and toolmaking allowed humans to punch far above our weight class, and working and living in groups made us less vulnerable to animals far more formidable than we are. Cooperation led to specialization, which anthropologists attribute to our dominant position in the animal kingdom.

Science writer Mark Maslin articulated this theory well: "A social brain also allows for the specialization of skills so individuals can concentrate on supporting childbirth, toolmaking, fire setting, hunting, or resource allocation. Humans have no natural weapons, but working in large groups and having tools allowed us to become the apex predator."

While there is (obviously) a huge upside for individuals who are able to successfully cooperate in the collective, those who are not will likely be ostracized, and individuals who are ostracized from the group are unlikely to survive and procreate. This cycle compounded over generations is likely to have been the evolutionary basis for our social compatibility. Maslin explains it likes this:

> Our social groups are large and complex, but this creates high stress levels for individuals because the rewards in terms of food, safety, and reproduction are so great. Hence, Oxford anthropologist Robin Dunbar argues our huge brain is primarily developed to keep track of rapidly changing relationships. It takes a huge amount of cognitive ability to exist in large social groups, and if you fall out of the group, you lose access to food and mates and are unlikely to reproduce and pass on your genes.

We are evolutionarily hardwired to be socially compatible, and this social instinct seems to have been the driving factor in the evolution of the human brain. Early hominids who were able to successfully cooperate and hone the social instinct survived and passed on their genes to subsequent generations. Those who were unable to did not. This cycle continued for two million years until we evolved into highly tuned social animals capable of complex cooperation.

Maslin suggested that being able to interpret and influence highly complex social interactions that involve a shifting landscape is what being smart really means. As he put it, "It is the detailed knowledge of society and the need to track and control the ever-changing relationship between people around us that has created our huge complex brain."

Yet despite the complexity of our brain, it is still just an organ that was produced by a unique set of evolutionary circumstances, and because it is optimized for those sets of circumstances, there are behaviors hardwired into us by evolution that are not compatible with being well-adjusted in modern society. Anxiety, fear, and ego played a crucial role in our survival on the savanna but don't help us navigate the wilderness of our modern lives.

Brains are not unique. Other animals also have brains that evolved to solve the challenges of their environment in unique ways. A mind, however, is a distinctively human quality. A mind is self-aware, recognizes its nature, and is capable of overcoming it. A mind is capable of denying itself the pleasure of the present in the pursuit of a better future.

As the philosopher Jean-Jacques Rousseau noted, an animal is governed completely by instinct, while man feels the call of instinct but realizes he is free to acquiesce or resist. Rousseau claimed that humans are distinguished from animals by the power of will and the consciousness of this power. If we accept this premise as true, then it stands to reason that in order for our better nature to reign, our mind must govern our brain. Though we know this to be true in theory, we have difficulty putting it into practice. As all things in life, it is far easier to say than to actually do. How then can we begin to rein in our brains?

In the moment between first impression to a stimulus and reaction lies transcendence. Our initial physical impression, what could be described as a feeling, is in large part involuntary. We perceive something, have a knee-jerk reaction to it, and that elicits a physical feeling (fear, anger, sadness, etc.). But what comes next—the subtler felt but longer lasting underlying emotion—depends largely on how we choose to interpret events. This interpretation of events and the subsequent actions we take as a result become the totality of our lives.

Our interpretation of events determines our actions. Our actions, in turn, define our self-narrative, and our self-narrative determines our emotions. It is essential then that we use our emotions as a barometer for right action. Actions that are congruent with who we are and our mission in life feel rewarding. Actions that are rewarding beget more actions of a similar ilk. Each of those actions, when properly directed, is a step on the path to mastery of our personal and professional lives. Mastery across life's key domains leads to harmony, and harmony leads to happiness.

Achieving an internal equilibrium from which we are our best selves is the goal, and this requires constant introspection and analysis. Objective analysis does not come to us naturally, but impressions do. In order for the mind to separate impression from reaction, we must work to strengthen our ability to overcome our impulses.

Developing this ability is a prerequisite to achieving our true aspirations and personal victory. The necessity of satisfying this requirement is what Munenori was relaying to his warriors when he wrote, "Devising stratagems within closed camp curtains, victory is determined a thousand miles away. There is an essential meaning for application of this verse to the martial arts and that is to understand the interior of the camp curtains to be your mind."

In order for our mind to govern our brain we must develop a strategy (that is, a systematic approach to the cultivation of our mind), and later, for our mind to effectively mold reality, we must develop a systematic approach to our daily affairs. When we cultivate anything, a plant, a skill, or a mind, it requires a great deal of persistence, patience, and presence.

3
PERSISTENCE
(ICHINEN)

"Nothing is impossible. With single-minded resolve (ichinen), heaven and earth can be moved as one pleases."

— *Yamamoto Tsunetomo*

Most undertakings are great undertakings. Creating a thriving business, raising a happy family, producing a work of art, or rising to the top of a particular field are just a few examples of common endeavors that take years and in some cases decades to execute. Regardless of which mountain we choose to climb, it will require persistence—the most fundamental part of the equation, the launching pad for our ascent.

Fundamental and essential yet often ignored. Most of us choose instant gratification over disciplined action that we know would bring delayed gratification manifold. Why? Because our instincts tell us to seek comfort and avoid pain.

Our instincts tell us that we have done enough. They tell us to stay in place, where it is comfortable, safe, and familiar, which makes sense from a survival standpoint when we take into consideration the conservation of energy and the avoidance of unnecessary dangers. However, the ability to overcome this instinct is a unique faculty of the human mind, which we must hone if we hope to leave our imprint on reality.

Our brain has a network of interacting regions that neuroscientists have dubbed the Default Mode Network (DMN). The DMN allows us to extrapolate into the future and predict how our actions may impact sequences of events. By acting on these predictions we come to understand how we can guide events in our favor and gain a belief in our agency.

Persistence is the cumulative repetition of this singular action; it amounts to overriding our evolutionary impulses and simply forcing ourselves to do something we may not want to do, over and over again for the sake of the bigger picture, the delayed reward. In doing so we literally rewire our brain and change the neurochemistry associated with our behavior.

I witnessed the rewiring of behavior firsthand. Prior to jujitsu I was plagued by inconsistency. Inconsistency in my work, in my relationships, in my physical conditioning, and in my diet. Forcing myself to do the hard thing, for an extended period of time, proved impossible, which, led to chronic mediocrity in all of my endeavors.

My force of will was weak. I always knew, as most of us do, what the right course of action was, and occasionally, I would even take it, but I never stayed on that path. I may have begun with gusto, but that effort petered out after a few weeks or months.

Why? Because persistence is hard, and difficulty threatened the false self-narrative I had created. Rather than accept that I was terrible at something, or weak, or unhealthy, I'd invent reasons that I failed at that thing or didn't need to excel at it. The need to protect a false narrative is fueled by our ego.

Ego clouds our judgment and makes us quit difficult tasks in the hopes that we may preserve our distorted self-image. Shedding that distorted self-image and the constant narration that accompanies it (in other words, overcoming the ego) is an essential precondition to the evolution of self. Overcoming the ego (and the rest of our adverse biological programing) requires persistence, which in turn requires a great deal of patience and humility.

PATIENCE (KANNIN)

> "If a man is prepared to accept a loss from the outset,
> he cannot be beaten. In this sense, if you are patient
> (kannin) you will not lose."
> — *Yamamoto Tsunetomo*

Patience (in this sense) equates to simply enduring loss, both big and small, with equanimity. Every loss brings information and opportunity for improvement. Every loss is a gift for advancement. By learning from defeat, we are greatly improved by it, and this improvement, if given a long enough time line, ensures our inevitable victory.

But can we handle loss? Can we really handle that embarrassing, gut-wrenching shame we feel when things don't go our way? Especially when things don't go our way repeatedly? Can we stay calm amid the chaos and keep a long-term perspective in the face of short-term defeats?

The reason we feel the sting of loss so severely is because it comes unexpectedly. We expect everything to work out.

We work hard, try our best, and become disillusioned when things don't go our way. Then we quit. Expectations prevent us from absorbing the information contained within losses that are necessary for advancement. They prevent us from receiving the profits of our pain.

By removing expectations and entering the fray again and again, we inch closer to victory with each defeat. Patience, time, and proper perspective allow the winning strategy to be revealed to us. But it can only be revealed to us if we are able to receive the message. If expectations lead to disappointment, ego clouds our vision.

Behind the fog of ego all obstacles look insurmountable. The only way to surmount the insurmountable is with the road map we are given by the losses we take. That road map can only be read if the narrator in your head (your ego) is silenced.

What is ego?

Ego is a by-product of the social instinct ingrained in us by evolution. It is how we see ourselves in the tribal hierarchy and our perceived value and worth within that hierarchy. The DMN, the same neural network that allows us to extrapolate into the future, also causes us to ruminate about past events and interpret them from a subjective (egotistical) perspective.

The inability to avoid this historical and future narrative is what Buddhists ironically call the monkey mind. The monkey mind (a part of our ego) finds sustenance in the subjective interpretation of the narrative we've constructed and our concern about our position in that imagined hierarchy.

Our ego tells us that we must feed it, that we must reinforce the necessity of our role in the hierarchy, lest we be put out to pasture. This monologue distorts the way we see the world. It constructs a narrative that exists only in our mind. Finding tranquility requires us to overcome this false narrative.

That is what Suzuki Shōsan, the fierce samurai warrior who would go on to become a famous Zen monk, was touching upon when he wrote, "When you manage to overcome your own mind, you overcome myriad concerns, rise above all things, and are free. When you are overcome by your own mind, you are burdened by myriad concerns, subordinate to things, unable to rise above."

Overcoming the false narrative that ego creates is akin to a cleansing of the mind. It amounts to making a switch in perspective from subjective to objective and removing ourselves from the equation. Shōsan also said, "There are myriad different methods of practice, but essentially they amount to no more than overcoming thoughts of yourself. The source of suffering is ego, the thought of self."

The sense of freedom I felt on the tatami mat was precisely this. A momentary respite from the shackles of self. Ego is a constant impediment in jujitsu. Loss, for practitioners at every level, is a frequent occurrence. When we're tired, distracted, injured, or just outclassed, we get beat, sometimes by those who are smaller, weaker, and less experienced.

When we incur these losses, there is always the temptation to write them off to fatigue, or distraction, or, you fill in the blank. The other option, the only real option, is to examine the flaws in our technique and work to fix them. These improvements can be judged objectively by our ability to avoid or exploit that flaw in our next roll.

It was not until I let go and stopped keeping score that I was able to improve in jujitsu. In the beginning I would avoid training with partners who could easily dominate me. Instead I'd look to roll with others whom I knew I could beat. As you can imagine, no real improvement was made. When I let go and accepted that I was going to lose, time and time again before I would win, I was able to improve.

I looked for challenging opponents, and every time I got submitted, I'd take notes. What did I get caught in, what was the sequence that led to that submission, and what moves could I employ to counter that attack or position? Then, in my next private class or drill session with a training partner, I'd work on improving that specific aspect of my game and, over time, I began to fix the many, many holes in my game.

It became easier to escape when I was mounted or an opponent took my back, joint locks became less menacing, every adverse position became an opportunity to work on my defense. Because I had drilled defense so much, it became second nature to me. My body instinctively knew what to do when caught in a bad position.

Then I started to improve my offense as well. When an attack sequence would fail, I'd break down the movements and find out why. Where in the attack did the opponent escape or shut down my offense? What worked, what didn't, and what needed to improve? Then, I would drill that choke or sweep or sequence, over and over again, until it too became second nature.

My improvement was a direct result of obtaining the objective perspective that Shōsan described earlier. By shutting off my false, self-defeating narrative and just accepting what was, I was able to see where my game was lacking and adjust accordingly. I would not have been able to improve if I had allowed my distorted self-image to cloud my judgment by couching my failures in excuses.

Muting our internal narrative and being present with reality is an essential requirement for improvement in any arena. Yet most of us constantly interject our feelings onto situations, thereby clouding reality. This prevents us from seeing things as they are and renders us incapable of taking effective action to get what we really want.

How then can we effectively remove ourselves from the equation?

The path to becoming our ideal selves begins with consistent and honest introspection. Without the proper perspective that honest introspection brings, we can't take the right action. As Ichijo Kaneyoshi noted, "Honesty just means a straightforward mind. If the mind is distorted, all behavior is distorted."

Distorted behavior is the product of a distorted mind, and a distorted mind is the product of the blinding narrative we construct to protect our fragile ego. Objective observation, on the other hand, requires a buoyant mind that is elastic, adaptive, and accommodating to all situations and can therefore discern the truth, regardless of the circumstances it finds itself in.

Takuan Soho, the Zen monk whose writing would inspire generations of samurai, used a common Buddhist metaphor to describe this state of mind. He wrote, "It is like a ball riding a swift-moving current: we respect the mind that flows on like this and does not stop for an instant in any place."

Buoyancy of mind is most needed and hardest to achieve in the midst of difficult circumstances. The wilder the river, the harder we find it to float. We exhaust ourselves trying to swim against the current rather than using its force to propel our action.

The perspective that a buoyant mind enables allows us to make objective observations and take effective action and, in doing so, overcome adverse circumstances. As Shōsan noted, "There are buoyant attitudes that overcome things, and depressive attitudes overcome by things."

If developing a buoyant mind is essential to accomplishing our mission, how can we cultivate this buoyancy?

5

BUOYANCY OF MIND (ZANSHIN)

"Ordinary people are those who take the falsehood of
illusions to be true, produce a selfish mind attached
to what has form, develop greedy, angry, and ignorant
thoughts, create all sorts of afflictions and lose
their basic mind, always distracted, overcome by
thoughts as they occur, racking their brains and
belaboring their bodies, without buoyancy of mind,
vainly passing the time benighted, alienated from
themselves and fixated on things."

— Suzuki Shōsan

"Things" are objects of the ego's desire (recognition, material possessions, a trophy wife, are but a few examples). A desire for "things" stems from an inability to overcome the internal monologue that ego creates, what Shōsan described as "the falsehood of illusion."

Because we have not yet overcome this monologue, we fail to define our true aspirations and are easily distracted by our ego's false, subjective interpretation of events and the subsequent desires that interpretation produces.

We do not have an internal road map by which we can measure our progress or lens through which we can interpret events objectively, so we let this false interpretation of events guide us and actively seek to obtain the objects of our ego's desire—things.

The attainment of things alienates us further from our ideal self and is always a hollow pursuit. The ego is never satisfied and never satiated. When we attain one object of the ego's desire, another takes its place. By blindly chasing after these desires, we are tossed about in a sea of uncertainty, constantly striving for a new object, with no end in sight.

This is what Shōsan was touching upon when he wrote, "If you are weak-minded, with thoughts fixating on things, the army of demons will gain strength, increase in power, and immediately invade the citadel of your real essence and confound your mind-king."

Our real essence is our ideal self and our mind-king is what samurai (and Buddhists) call the basic mind, a mind that is empty, and as such, is free from a self-defeating narrative. The army of demons is the noise, distraction, and resistance that are heir to modern life and the enemy of tranquility.

Without buoyancy of mind we become distracted by the pursuit of things and find ourselves in complex situations that bring us no fulfillment. The army of demons confines our mind-king and noise reigns supreme. When the mind is not fixated on things, however, it can define and seek to manifest its purpose. Purpose, and progress toward that purpose, lead to happiness.

Buoyancy of mind is simply mental fluidity that is the result of unbroken focus. Focus requires presence of mind, and presence of mind requires peace of mind. Peace of mind allows us to maintain the mental fluidity needed to achieve a proper perspective. By maintaining that peace of mind and the presence it brings, we create a protective barrier between us and circumstance, and that distance allows us to remain unmarred by the ugliness of the life that we will inevitably encounter as we actively seek to direct its course.

Yagyū Munenori highlighted the advantage of this distance: "The man who has been able to pacify his mind once and for all and from beginning to end can mingle with the dust of the world and remain unstained. Though he moves through the world all day long, he himself is unmovable."

Having peace of mind is a prerequisite to achieving mental fluidity, which leads to rational decisions and right action. On the other hand, a perturbed mind is highly irrational. Objectively speaking, none of us would leave critical decisions to another person who was clearly in psychological distress. You wouldn't want a schizophrenic piloting an airplane, for example. Why? Because we recognize that a schizophrenic is out of touch with the reality that the rest of us are experiencing and that their ability to reason is clouded by the narrative in their head that only they can hear. Sound familiar?

Thus, to be able to achieve the unbroken focus that is buoyancy of mind, the mind itself must first be calm. This is especially true in times of turmoil. If you can achieve peace of mind when others are perturbed, you can see what they can't. This is a weapon of perception and an advantage to be exploited. Shiba Yoshimasa noted, "For warriors in particular, if you calm your own mind and discern the inner minds of others, that may be called the foremost art of war."

Discerning the inner mind of others is a crucial component of discovering the hidden mechanisms that govern the circumstances we find ourselves in, and it is an exercise in perception that I will touch on in the coming chapters. Calming your own mind, however, boils down to overcoming fear. Overcoming fear amounts to taking disciplined action to find and sever the root of our fear.

We choose what we do with fear. It can either be a prison or fuel for our ascent. Hirayama Heigen suggested that this singular decision determines whether we will be successful in all of our endeavors. He wrote, "Victory and defeat are not in relative skill; courage or cowardice make the difference. The courageous are unafraid, so they're able to concentrate completely, without distraction. That is how they secure their victories."

The enemy of inner peace wears many masks but has only one face, a myriad of different forms but one root, fear. When we let fear play a leading role in our narrative, it stifles our opportunities because we fail to see them or fail to act. Lost opportunities in turn fuel our fear of further loss, thus creating a self-perpetuating, parasitic cycle, with us as its host.

Far from being an unwilling host, our ego welcomes the parasitic cycle because it creates an excuse for our failures, a justification for the insurmountable obstacles of our own making. We tell ourselves that other people will understand why we came up short and allow that narrative to become reality rather than looking for angles to remake reality.

Anxiety is perhaps the most common and most egregious manifestation of fear because of its consistent nature. Water, one of the softest substances on earth, can cut canyons through mountains because of its continual flow. In much the same way, continual thoughts spread across many mental cycles become patterns. These patterns of thoughts become patterns of behavior and patterns of behavior, our actions, define us and become us.

If anxiety (low intensity, high duration fear) is allowed to carve its course through our mind, it creates a canyon of negativity. A canyon that other thoughts will inevitably fall into and be consumed by. The more we feed the canyon, the bigger it grows until it dominates our perception entirely.

We feel a low-level fear in ordinary situations. Our biological responses become disharmonies with our reality. We feel stress when we shouldn't. Ordinary life becomes a daunting task. We lose sight of the miracle of existence and are blind to the gifts of the ordinary. We forget to enjoy the ride and take in the scenery, and, instead, we are tormented by each bump along the long and winding road of life.

We quite literally lose our minds, or better said, we lose control of our minds. This leads to paralysis because fear in any form inhibits proper analysis and impedes effective action. Overcoming this aspect of our perception, however, is far easier said than done.

Our brains are hardwired to be gripped by fear. Fear is a well-honed survival instinct ingrained into us by millions of years of evolution. It demands all of our immediate attention and offers no room for other thoughts. What we experience when we experience fear is an instinctual recognition of a potential threat to our well-being and the physiological reaction that follows, which forces the mind to dedicate all of its faculties to resolving the issue by pacifying the potential danger— obscure as that so-called danger may be.

Anxiety is an extension of that hardwiring. It is fear extrapolated into the future, or fear of future events. Fear manifests itself as anxiety when there is no perceivable solution to the obstacles our imagination creates or, worse, when we are not actively working toward those solutions.

The mind, though we may try to put it elsewhere, keeps working on the unsolved problem, regardless of the setting it finds itself in. Thus, we begin to ruminate about past or future events, and our thoughts seemingly take on a life of their own. We are not in control of our thoughts. Instead, our emotional state is at the mercy of a frightened and consequently irrational mind.

The irony is that most things we fear never come to pass. As Tsunetomo wrote, "Calamities are usually not as bad as anticipated beforehand, it is foolhardy to feel anxiety about tribulations not yet endured."

I've had a crippling relationship with anxiety my entire life. Fear has been a dominant emotion for as long as I can remember. I had a tumultuous childhood, which led to fears of abandonment and rejection when I was younger. As I got older, those fears morphed into existential fear, a crisis of purpose, which, in turn, caused a crisis of confidence.

Insecurity and self-doubt reigned supreme. This self-doubt was compounded by a contradictory internal drive that I believe each one of us has, to fulfill our true purpose. Deep down inside, I knew that I wasn't doing my life's work, and this realization tore at the fabric of my soul. At the same time, I was scared of the judgment that failure would bring.

These contradicting motivations led to a contradiction in myself that could be sensed by others. My actions and my motivations were not in congruence, and consequently sincerity and passion were missing from my life. Insecurity in my person caused me to project insecurity onto situations and relationships, which became a self-fulfilling prophecy.

In relationships (both platonic and romantic) I was needy, fearful of being abandoned, of not being good enough, of ending up old and alone. And much like clutching a fistful of sand, the harder I'd cling to it, the faster it would dissappear.

I let this fear cripple me for the better part of three decades. I was frozen, a slave to biological impulses I could not overcome. The instinctual pull was just too strong (or so I thought).

We already know that it is incumbent upon us for ascension from our lower selves to override our biological impulses. Fear in all its forms is just another biological impulse that must be tamed. As such, there are exercises that have been proven to have tangible benefits in quelling fear and pacifying our monkey mind.

Meditation is an effective vehicle for overcoming anxiety and generally quieting the mind. In fMRI scans of the brain, expert meditators actually showed a decrease in activity in the DMN, essentially overriding their evolutionary impulses through training. Exercises in perception (like journaling) are another effective way of training the mind to push through fear and work best when accompanied by the stillness that meditation brings. This routine gives the mind both the distance and space needed to frame events in their proper context.

For me, meditation creates the distance needed to gain the clarity that leads to right action. It widens that small interval between impression and reaction. Through meditation I've come to recognize that I don't have to act on every impulse or indulge every thought. I (whatever part of me is observing the observer) can elect which thoughts to identify with and which to let go. I don't have to believe every impression or yield to every emotion. This distance allows me to frame events in their proper context, which, in turn, allows me to choose the right course of action.

Framing events in their proper context amounts to simply looking at events without fear or expectations. By accepting the negative consequences of an action as inevitable, we mitigate our expectations and lose our fear of those consequences.

Tsunetomo accurately encapsulates this mindset with the following allegory: "There is a lesson to be learned from a downpour of rain. If you get caught in a sudden cloudburst, you will still get a drenching even though you try to keep dry by hurrying along and taking cover under overhangs of roofs. If you are prepared to get wet from the start, the result is still the same but there is no hardship. This attitude can be applied to all things."

Four hundred years after this was written, corporate America has put this principle into practice in an exercise known as the premortem. Prior to launch, companies look at their latest product, service, or venture as if it failed and then dissect the factors that led to that failure. This is meant to prevent blunders but also helps the parties involved accept failure as an inevitable part of their path. We too can apply this exercise to our own lives by simply accepting the negative consequences of an action as inevitable.

Prior to embarking on a course of action, imagine that the things that can go wrong will, then ask yourself if you can handle the consequences. Examine the things you fear thoroughly. Strip them to their base and see them for what they really are. What is it that you are afraid of and how bad is it upon closer inspection?

The circumstances we think are fatal are often just flesh wounds. Temporary unemployment, a damaged reputation, severely depleted finances, the end of a long romantic relationship, and the loss of a loved one all feel like the end of the world, but they aren't. Fate is fluid and pain is temporary. Temporary pain becomes chronic when prolonged with prescription medication, alcohol, drugs, self-destructive behavior, lethargy, junk food, and so on.

On the other hand, if we are prepared to accept the consequences for calculated actions deliberately taken, then life will never find us unprepared for its hurdles. Expected bumps bring no pain when we meet them unflinchingly.

When we meet with hardship resolutely, time and time again, life becomes easier. The answer to how much can we bear becomes more every time. Consequences that seemed like a death sentence before, now begin to lose their gravity. Our actions become bolder, our skin grows thicker, and our lives get better. We can walk calmly in the rain if we have no fear of getting wet.

As we have already learned, victory is secured by investing in repetitive defeat. We can only lose so many times before we win. The bolder the actions we take, the greater our inevitable victory will be. Silence fear and doubt through analysis and action.

The irony is that, by accepting the horrible event as inevitable, we push it further away through sober, lucid thinking, which can only be done in the absence of fear. This is what Heigen meant when he wrote, "On a field of battle, he who becomes absorbed in inevitable death will survive without trying to stay alive."

This lucidness and absence of fear comes from first making peace with circumstance—circumstances that will never find us unprepared because we have analyzed potential outcomes, especially the negative ones, and have determined that we can handle them. Being aware of the totality of events allows our mind to be truly fluid, since we are not married to a particular set of circumstances. Takuan Soho described it like this: "The mind of the man who has arrived does not stop at one thing even for a bit. It is like pushing down the gourd in the water."

If suffering is born of attachment, then the mind that is attached to things will suffer greatly because all things are constantly in flux. Things do not have to be things in the material sense, they can be a commonly accepted way of doing things, like religious beliefs, or perceived scientific truths, for example. All of these have and will change throughout the course of human history, as unfathomable as this may be to us today.

Yet if the mind is buoyant and not married to a set of circumstances, it can see each moment clearly and accommodate itself accordingly. Instead of being a prisoner to the past and wishing that things could be the way they once were, the buoyant mind shifts effortlessly from one moment to the next.

Armed with this fluidity, the mind can begin to shape reality, much like flowing water can carve solid rock. When our mind is guided by a clear purpose and we consistently mold circumstances to bring that vision into fruition, we create a path to reaching our goal, and though the mind itself is buoyant, the object of its action remains constant. This consistency of purpose becomes our way, our path, and comes to define us.

6

THE WAY

Articulating and actuating our purpose (finding and walking our path) is a process that is unique to each of us and one we must master if we hope to find harmony in our lives. Fortunately, the advent of the internet has created plentiful opportunities for us to find our path and a multitude of ways by which we can travel it.

In order to know what we want, however, we must first define our values, our abilities, and our interests; then we can use them as guideposts on the path to discovering our purpose. Defining our values, abilities, and interests forces us to articulate what it is we care about, enjoy doing, and derive a sense of meaning from.

Keith Ferrazzi, the author and entrepreneur, describes this intersection as the blue flame: "We all have our own loves, insecurities, strengths, weaknesses, and unique capabilities. And we have to take those into account in figuring out where our talents and desires intersect. That intersection is what I call your blue flame, where passion and ability come together. When that blue flame is ignited within a person, it is a powerful force in getting you where you want to be."

It is from the intersection of these talents and interests that Ferrazzi claims we find meaning and create value.

I've always known what my blue flame was. Ever since I read Goosebumps in elementary school, I've known that I wanted to a be a writer, but fear, noise, distraction, and chasing objects of the ego's desire kept me from my path. Yet no matter how hard I tried, I couldn't quench the yearning to create.

Everything else I did in life felt false, like a hollow charade. And when we are playing a part, we can never truly be sincere. This lack of sincerity kept me from excelling at anything, which, in turn, kept me from experiencing the joy of a job well done and the confidence we can derive from that—the cumulative effect of which builds character.

It wasn't until I was forced by life events, detailed in a later chapter, to abandon my business and pursue writing (and to some extent marketing) full-time that I was able to experience the same sense of freedom I felt on the tatami mats, outside of the gym.

I began to feel that same sense of freedom at my desk. When writing, like practicing jujitsu, I was completely present. My mind wasn't and didn't wish to be elsewhere. It was completely immersed in resolving the issue at hand and consequently was content.

Immersion is what all of our paths have in common. Regardless of how we find our way, and unique as it may be, immersing ourselves in the pursuit of our purpose creates a sense of freedom, and that same sense of freedom is felt by every person who walks their true path. Because when we are fully immersed in the moment, we're free, free from fear, from worry and from doubt, and instead we are fully present, engaged, and alive.

This is often referred to as a flow state. A flow state is a term coined in 1975 by psychologist Mihály Csíkszentmihályi and can be described as "the mental state of operation in which a person performing an activity is fully immersed in a feeling of energized focus, full involvement, and enjoyment in the process of the activity."

We have all experienced this sense of immersion when we lose ourselves in a book, a sunset, a game, or a task. In this state, we are free from the noise that animates our monkey mind. Freedom from worry leads to enjoyment from which we can derive meaning if the flow state is properly directed to reach our larger goals.

In other words, if we have accurately articulated our purpose, we can lose ourselves in the pursuit of that purpose and derive meaning from the immersion. Extrapolated across a long enough time line, a series of repetitive flow states, when combined with a proper perspective and guided by an overarching vision toward a grand goal, becomes the formula for a fulfilling life.

If you have not yet found your path, search for instances of immersion. What activities cause you to lose yourself in energized focus and bring you fulfillment? Which of those activities is constructive to you and others and is aligned with your abilities and your values? Can that intersection become your purpose, your life's purpose?

The flow state we find ourselves in time and time again in the pursuit of our purpose is truly, as Suzuki Shōsan said, "a way into the deep via the shallow." However, this sense of immersion need not be limited to the pursuit of our purpose. Our seemingly shallow, everyday experience is an opportunity for us to transcend to higher planes of consciousness through complete immersion.

Shōsan expands on this idea. He wrote, "Be aware that this stable, firm attitude is itself meditation practice. There is no other method of concentration to seek. Even Buddhahood itself is just a matter of applying full attention steadily, without being disturbed by things. Developing a confident attitude that is never pained or vexed or worried or saddened or altered or frightened."

Developing a confident attitude through immersion is a practice that is best honed by executing ordinary duties with excellence. The pursuit of excellence can and should be applied to every area of our life and, as such, there is divinity in the mundane.

We should not seek freedom from our responsibilities but rather freedom through them. Work especially, since it is the best training ground for optimizing our ability to shape reality. Far from being a burden, work is an opportunity to, as Shōsan wrote, "use the fierce and firm mind-sword to cut down the enemy of birth and death and live in great peace."

The enemy of peace is fear, which equates to a paralysis of the mind. Paralysis is incompatible with flow and conversely tranquility, both of which are necessary if we want to live a harmonious and fulfilling life. By immersing ourselves in experience, however, we free ourselves from this paralysis and use the mind-sword we forge in the fire of presence to cut through obstacles and create the harmony we seek.

Finding flow, however, requires us to struggle. Struggle in which we immerse ourselves (paradoxically) brings us peace and propels progress, which produces a belief in our own agency. This belief gives us confidence, a confidence others can sense and will admire, which further fuels our inner well-being, creating a self-perpetuating, positively reinforcing cycle that drives us to seek struggle and consequently find harmony.

Getting into the mental state where we can experience immersion regularly requires discipline, proper perspective, and a process of progressive mastery, which starts in one domain of life and bleeds into others.

We normally find flow in one area of our lives (whether it be an athletic, intellectual, professional, or artistic pursuit), but as we spend more time in that state, we begin to carry that same presence into other domains. Single-minded focus on the present moment becomes the mind's default mode after enough practice. This is what Takuan Soho was referring to when he wrote, "If one always approaches his mind in this way, at a later date it will suddenly come to this condition by itself."

Presence becomes a way of thinking, a hyperfocus on the present moment. And as Tsunetomo noted, hyperfocus is the mental state we should seek to achieve in all of our affairs: "There is surely nothing other than the single purpose of the present moment. A man's whole life is a succession of moment after moment. If one fully understands the present moment, there will be nothing else to do, and nothing else to pursue. Live being true to the single purpose of the moment."

If life is nothing more than one moment after the next and we are fully immersed in each moment, then the sum total of those moments is a fulfilling life. What Tsunetomo is preaching is the gospel of immersion.

When you are immersed, the process of mastery becomes its own reward. When we are not focused on the fruits of our labor and instead are immersed in the process, the labor becomes its own fruit. The irony of this is that the tangible rewards our ego desires come most often to those who love their labor.

Samurai call this mindset of immersion single-mindedness. Tsunetomo wrote of single-mindedness, "When one understands this settling into single-mindedness well, his affairs will thin out."

What he means is that when we apply this mindset of immersion to different areas of our life, those areas get better. When this mindset of immersion becomes our default mode and thoughts fall away entirely, we have attained an imperturbable mind. Attaining an imperturbable mind is our end goal, the collective destination where all our singular paths lead.

7

THE IMPERTURBABLE MIND

"Not stopping the mind is object and essence.
Put nowhere, it will be everywhere."
—*Yagyū Munenori*

The imperturbable mind is a buoyant mind that has been subjected to years of training and has become so elastic that it uses thoughts to transgress thinking. Not simply accommodating itself to any scenario but rather removing itself entirely. It is from this place of emptiness that decisions can be reached with alacrity seemingly instantaneously.

As such, the imperturbable mind is often referred to as and is synonymous with No Mind. No Mind, meaning a lack of thoughts. No Mind is something we've all witnessed in high-level athletes. Their movements flow without premeditation.

They react effortlessly to the situation at hand; their body seems to be working independently of their conscious mind. There is no time for contemplation, no space between stimulus and action. They flow effortlessly from one moment to the next. Taking whatever stance is called for that moment and the next they're somewhere else, creating new forms and patterns, dancing with time and space to a rhythm of their making.

We can only arrive at this state after first achieving a technical mastery of a given domain, then transforming that technique into fluid creativity and, in doing so, leaving technique behind. Munenori explains this succinctly: "When you have run the length of various practices and none of those practices remain in your mind, that very lack of mind is itself the heart of all things.... By forgetting about training and casting off your mind you will be all the more unaware of yourself. The place you come to in this way is the perfection of the way. At this level you enter through training and arrive at its very absence."

Through rigorous discipline practitioners achieve technical mastery of a specific domain. In doing so, the ego is subdued over and over again, which makes ego pacification second nature after enough training. In this state, the mind is empty and devoid of form.

From this place of formlessness, the mind is free to mold itself to the situation at hand. To become whatever is needed instantly and effortlessly. Munenori wrote about this paradoxical relationship: "When the mind does not move it is emptiness, when emptiness moves it is mind."

The opposite of this is fixation. When the mind becomes fixated on an object or end it loses sight of the many moving pieces that comprise reality, thereby pushing that object or end further away. Munenori describes this as a congealing of the mind: "If the mind congeals in one place and remains with one thing, it is like frozen water and is unable to be used freely: ice that can wash neither hands nor feet. When the mind is melted and is used like water, extending throughout the body, it can be sent wherever one wants to send it."

As we've already learned, this congealing (i.e., fixation) is caused by a discontinuity between our expectations and reality. We fixate on the way things should be or how they were, rather than how they are. This discontinuity distracts us from the present. It prevents us from seeing the conditions for improvement and paralyzes our actions.

In jujitsu, when I fixate on victory it almost always leads to defeat. The veneer of expectations colors reality falsely and I expect to win or dominate my opponent. Perhaps because I have in a previous match or roll. When I inevitably find myself in a nondominant or defensive position my mind fails to adapt to reality and instead is stuck, disappointed, congealed in the past, unable to think clearly, and, as such, easy to beat.

On the other hand, when our mind is free from a distracting narrative and has a deep reservoir of technical knowledge to draw upon and transform, the mind, the body, and the subconscious work together, producing effortless action.

I have by no means achieved an imperturbable mind, but I have had brief moments of imperturbability on the mats and in my life. My greatest victories in jujitsu have come when I thought I was going to lose. When I was competing against or rolling with a more advanced opponent. All expectation of victory gone, my mind was free to focus all of its faculties on the moment at hand.

Every time I was caught in a compromising position, my body instinctively knew how to escape. The mind, and the myriad of thoughts and sensations that accompany the self (pain, fatigue, and even strategy), weren't present. Thoughts were absent all together. My training, however, was very much present; my movements were technical and efficient, but they weren't guided by my conscious mind.

It was effortless action, much like flowing water. There was no position to which I could not accommodate myself and ultimately turn to my advantage. This mental imperturbability lead to fluid combat, which, after enough time, would frustrate my opponent. Frustrated, unable to focus entirely, they would make a mistake which my mind, undistracted, fully focused, and energized, could then seize.

Effortless action is the product of years of progressive mastery, what samurai called kaizen. Our goal, like theirs, is to achieve an imperturbable mind through technical proficiency by moving beyond it. This shift, from buoyancy to imperturbability, marks the transition from technician to master, says Adachi Masahiro: "A master is a technician with an imperturbable mind."

Moving beyond technical proficiency, however, requires us to first be technically proficient. The act of acquiring technical proficiency requires us to engage fully with the task at hand and then to repeat that immersive action day in and day out for years on end.

The daily repetition of single-minded focus across a long enough time line allows us to achieve a state of clear presence from which we are able to peer into the hidden principles of the things that constitute our existence. Understanding these principles, how things work without the artifice, is vital to attaining the clarity of vision needed to complete our mission.

8

SEEING BENEATH THE SURFACE

"You must observe the situation clearly and with great intensity. This is the great principle of the martial arts."
— *Yagyū Munenori*

Understanding the principle of things equates to discovering the hidden mechanisms that govern the circumstances that comprise our reality. Discovering these mechanisms requires us to dig beneath the surface of seemingly ordinary events and observe their inner workings with the detached intensity of a buoyant mind.

Legendary swordsman Miyamoto Musashi articulated the distinction between surface level perception and a deeper understanding of events when he wrote, "Observation and perception are two separate things; the observing eye is stronger, the perceiving eye is weaker."

The observing eye is the lens through which we must examine our world. It is devoid of self (that is, the narrator or interpreter of events) and therefore is not subject to the same emotional distortions as the perceiving eye. The very act of perceiving necessitates that there be a narrator, someone, or thing to perceive. We've come to understand that the narrator is our ego, and when our ego is present, it distorts reality, rendering us incapable of taking effective action.

When we shut the narration off and observe events with single-minded focus instead, we can pick up on subtle details that give us a window into their inner workings. We begin to understand how things really function beneath the surface. The process of discovering governing principles through rigorous, detached observation and investigation is an art that can be applied across life's different domains.

Describing this process, Munenori said, "Having no conflicts in association with friends from beginning to end is also a matter of seeing into the principle of a relationship and this too is a martial art of the mind … Arranging objects in your living room is a matter of using what is right for each place and this too is a matter of seeing into the principles of those places. This is not unlike the very heart of martial arts. The arena may change but the principle remains the same."

Perceiving these hidden mechanisms at work in different arenas is what I call theory, and the application of that theory is what I call technique. It is important to note that knowledge is not always (and perhaps not even most often) acquired in a linear theory to technique trajectory. In what the philosopher Nassim Nicholas Taleb calls convex tinkering, knowledge often comes from tinkering with and improving upon existing systems or forms of knowledge that lead to new discoveries. The discoverers may in fact be ignorant of the science. We often understand how to do something long before we understand why it works.

Think about the hidden mechanism at work in making wine, cheese, or bread. All of these were made centuries (and in some cases millennia) before microbes and bacteria were understood. Despite lacking a fundamental knowledge of biology, early artisans had a tertiary understanding of the hidden mechanisms at work, which was sufficient to not only make but master the art of making wine, bread, cheese, and so on. In much the same way artisans of old could master culinary cultivation without fully understanding the process, so too can we, through mastery, make art of our lives without fully understanding the mysteries of existence.

Peering into hidden principles is a vital part of the process by which we acquire wisdom and is the seed of our species' insight. As individuals we must peer into the principles of the things that govern our own lives, too, if we wish to achieve an understanding of and a degree of agency over events, the totality of which constitutes our lives.

Peering into the principles of jujitsu and examining which aspects of the art gave me that serene sense of progress led me to find my path outside of the gym. I recognized, as discussed earlier, that the flow state I found myself in on the mats could also be found in creative pursuits, and that writing professionally, like jujitsu, would be accompanied by a myriad of challenges that I would have to face incrementally for a lifetime. But the act of overcoming these challenges was and is its own reward. That insight came from taking the context of the lessons I learned in one domain and applying them to another.

That act of perceiving hidden mechanisms at work is something we all do instinctively when we converse. We read body language and tone to decipher what's really being said. Seeing beneath the surface is that same act applied to different domains. It amounts to examining the people and situations that come into our lives with cautious clarity to see what's going on beneath the surface and discovering what factors are actually motivating action or driving events.

With enough practice, peering into the principle of things becomes second nature, hidden mechanisms become visible to us, and a world of possibilities opens itself up to us. If we can see hidden mechanisms where others can't and use that vision to alter reality, we become innovators. This is true of artists, entrepreneurs, scientists, and creators of every ilk. Countless contributors to human wisdom pierced reality's veil and brought back insights that illuminated and elevated mankind.

But why do these mechanisms remain hidden to the rest of us? Because observing them is difficult. Most of us don't allocate the time or energy needed to carefully examine the situations we find ourselves in. Most of us are rushing from one moment to the next, toward some end goal we know naught (the end of the workday, retirement, death?). Few of us take a philosophical approach to daily affairs and examine situations and people with cautious clarity. Even fewer of us extend this cautious examination to our lives as a whole.

In rushing blindly from one moment to the next, we see only what is in front of us (often without clarity) and fail to see the bigger picture. We miss the forest for the trees, as the saying aptly goes.

In order to carve our path, we must peer into the hidden mechanism at work not only in the moment-to-moment happenings that govern our daily affairs but in the events that govern the broader world around us. By subjecting macro events to the same process of fluid examination that we subject our daily affairs to, we find ways to remake our reality over a prolonged period of time.

The process of subjecting macro affairs to micro examination is what Musashi was describing when he wrote, "In strategy it is important to see distant things as if they were close and to take a distanced view of close things. If you do not look at things on a large scale, it will be impossible for you to master strategy."

Munenori called this exercise in macro perception, "understanding the entire song." Understanding the entire song, as opposed to playing just one instrument, gives us a sense of security. Circumstances become less frightening when we can dissect them. If the song is not to our liking and we are able to discern which instrument is out of tune, the melody can be restored. If, however, we are deaf to the sound of instruments not our own, the melody becomes incoherent noise.

Understanding the entire song is not a matter of having mastery over every domain of life, much like an orchestra conductor is not a master of every instrument. Rather it is a matter of extending the principles we have learned in the micro to the macro. Musashi explained this succinctly: "The principle of strategy is having one thing, to know ten thousand things."

The process of looking into things, of discovering hidden mechanisms at work, becomes a process we can apply to larger domains where chains of events become highly unpredictable. The process of analysis and (fluid) action, when undertaken with a buoyant mind and directed toward a concrete goal, becomes effective strategy. Much like our mind, effective strategy is adaptable, but its aim remains constant.

Munenori explained this well. He said, "Exhaustively extending your knowledge generally means to know men as they are in the world and to exhaustively know the principles of all things. If you exhaustively know the principles of all things, there is nothing remaining unknown and nothing that cannot be done."

By understanding human nature and knowing how to discover the inner workings of things, we can figure out how to navigate almost every situation. Though the arena may change, the effectiveness of pristine analysis and fluid action do not.

The same can be said for the principles that ultimately lead to mastery. We learn the route to excellence by walking our own path and in doing so we come to understand all others. Though the domain may differ, the process does not. This is what Musashi meant when he wrote, "If you know the Way broadly, you will see it in all things. Men must polish their particular Way."

Polishing our particular way (pursuing our purpose) gives us clarity because we gain an intimate understanding of what is required to achieve excellence, and we can recognize this same process at work in exterior circumstances and other people.

The process of polishing our way boils down to progressive mastery. Progressive mastery is a long-term improvement process that requires us to first understand the hidden mechanisms governing a particular set of circumstances, then take decisive action based on our findings, objectively assess our progress, find and correct our shortcomings, and then repeat this process over and over again until the object of our action (our mission) is complete. (This incremental process is the exact trajectory my improvement in jujitsu followed.)

This improvement process becomes a methodology that we can apply to different domains of our life with great confidence because we know the winning formula, have applied it before, and are sure we can do it again. A good example of polishing an individual way that in turn illuminates all others is how Andy Grove, the legendary CEO of Intel and clear master of one domain (business), used the principles of pristine analysis and effective action to combat cancer.

In his book *Great by Choice*, Jim Collins and Morten T. Hansen detailed how Andy Grove reacted to the news that he had a tumor the size of a sugar cube growing in his prostate gland:

> In 1994, Andy Grove, chief executive of Intel, underwent a routine blood test that came back with a worrisome number: a PSA (prostate-specific antigen) reading of 5, indicating that there could be a tumor the size of a sugar cube growing inside his prostate gland. The doctor suggested that Grove's first step should be to visit the urologist. Most people would do exactly that, but that wasn't Andy Grove's response. Instead, he began reading research articles written by medical scientists for medical scientists. Grove delved into the data. What did the PSA test really indicate? How did the biochemistry work? What were the statistics of prostate cancer, and the pros and cons of treatment options? He also

decided to "test the tests" to validate the data in his readings, sending blood samples to separate labs to calibrate the degree of lab variation in the test. Only after all this did Grove make an appointment with the urologist.

But even then, Grove did not rely on his doctors to create a treatment plan. After an MRI and a bone scan, he embarked on a more extensive research regimen, going directly to original sources, culling through the primary data. He obtained all the articles cited in the bibliography of a prostate-cancer reference book, devoured those, then searched for scientific literature that had been published in the six to nine months after the publication of that book, and then obtained even more materials that'd been cited in those publications. Grove maintained an intense CEO schedule by day and his prostate research regimen by night, plotting data, cross-referencing different studies, and trying to make sense of it all. He learned through his research that there was a raging intellectual war over various cancer-treatment regimens. Grove realized he ultimately had to draw his own decision trees; plug in his own probability equations; and come to his own data-driven, logical conclusions about his treatment plan.

"As a patient whose life and well-being depended on a meeting of minds," he later wrote in *Fortune* magazine, "I realized I would have to do some cross-disciplinary work on my own." After electing to undergo a biopsy, which confirmed the presence of a moderately aggressive tumor, Grove threw his prodigious mental capacity at the question of what he should do next.

Cancer treatments usually involve some combination of slicing you up (surgery), frying you (radiation), or poisoning you (chemotherapy); and each option has its own side effects, consequences, and survival rates.

Furthermore, each doctor tends to have a bias toward a particular treatment, influenced by that doctor's own specialties (if you're a hammer, everything you see looks like a nail). Grove found proponents of traditional surgery, cryosurgery, external radiation, seed therapy, high-dose-rate radiation, and combination therapies. The dominant conventional wisdom pointed to surgery, but Grove's own direct engagement with the evidence led him to a different choice (a combination radiation therapy). In the end, Grove reflected, "I decided to bet on my own charts."

Now, you might be thinking, "My goodness, what an arrogant jerk! Who does he think he is to defy the whole medical establishment?" But think about it this way: Grove discovered that the medical establishment itself had great uncertainty and disagreement within its own ranks, a dynamic amplified by rapidly advancing technologies. Had Grove faced a broken arm, with no uncertainty about treatment and zero risk of death, he wouldn't have spent hundreds of hours building charts of data.

The analysis that leads to understanding requires a fundamental stillness that can only be achieved by an empty mind. Imagine the many fears that Grove had to silence in order to attain the proper perspective that led to the pristine analysis he was able to make and the effective action he was able to take as a result.

When the mind is empty, it's formless; formlessness, when combined with technical mastery, is the route to excellence. Excellence brings harmony. Finding harmony across life's many landscapes and seasons amounts to a fluid execution of this same process.

Suzuki Shōsan described it like this: "People who attain the Way know the principle of fundamental emptiness, use principle and duty as a forge to temper the mind day and night, get rid of the residue of impurities, make it a pure unhindered mind-sword, cut through the root of selfish and obsessive thoughts, overcome all thoughts, surmount everything, and are unfazed by anything, unborn and undying. These are called people of the Way."

People of the way (people who have developed an imperturbable mind) often have a strong yet soothingly subtle energy about them. Their presence feels deep as if they are connected to a different source. This is because the process of pristine analysis and effective action requires them to have a clear perspective at all times and in every situation.

Maintaining that clear perspective requires their mind to be formless, and formlessness necessitates emptiness. Water is often used as a metaphor (particularly in Taoism) when describing formlessness. Water takes the shape of any container it is put into. It can be liquid, ice or, vapor, but its essence remains the same.

In much the same way, formlessness manifested in human form allows its owner to be instantly at peace in every situation, comfortable under any circumstance, unmoved, though they themselves move through the world. Or as Shōsan defined it, "they overcome all thoughts, surmount everything, and are unfazed by anything," thus freeing their mind from the confines of birth and death (that is, they are unborn and undying).

As we have already learned, this peace of mind is what samurai called the imperturbable mind. It is also what Stoics aptly named the inner citadel. Regardless of how we choose to label it, it amounts to a tranquility that is independent of circumstance and is a state of mind that we should all aspire to attain. How then can we reach this state?

The imperturbable mind is a buoyant mind calloused by the grind of discipline. Discipline is but one facet of the samurai's moral code; thus having a moral code is a prerequisite to developing an imperturbable mind. If each of our paths leads to our own inner citadel, we must first pave the way with the principles and actions that build the character necessary for our mental evolution. As such, our moral code becomes indispensable to completing our mission.

MORAL CODE (NIGIRI)

SINCERITY

> "Nothing lacking sincerity has worth."
> *—Yamamoto Tsunetomo*

Sincerity is a by-product of honesty, and honesty is a prerequisite to good judgment, which leads to effective action that discipline forges into habit. This cycle doesn't work without sincerity. Sincerity is the difference between merely reading the words written in this book and walking your path.

When you are sincere about something, you exude an aura of authenticity that can be sensed by others. Insincerity, on the other hand, leads to negativity because it is a form of internal conflict that can also be sensed by others. We have all felt this internal conflict before. Working at a job we hate and being in a relationship that has passed its expiration date are but two common examples.

All forms of insincerity cause this emotional reaction in varying degrees. Feeling this way long enough causes us to be jaded and cynical and blinds us to the seemingly limitless possibilities that are in our reach. As a result, we come to believe that this feeling of disappointment is our standard emotional hue, devoid of fun, the fire from our youth gone.

Disappointment was my standard emotional hue until I found my path. It was my baseline for so long that I forgot what it was like to feel excitement and joy (outside of modern forms of escapism). I never put forth sincere effort (at anything) and, as a result, never got to experience the growth that leads to pride and builds character. I was instead merely being tossed around by life's events, with no ends to aspire to other than obtaining objects of the ego's desire.

This sort of purgatory is where most of us live our lives. But it doesn't have to be. When we're sincere, we're honest, and when we are honest with ourselves, we can begin to decipher what we really want and dissect the factors keeping us from attaining those goals. From this place of internal alignment, we can make great effort without self-confliction and in doing so make the effort, effortless.

This is because when you are truly sincere about something, laboring on behalf of that something becomes enjoyable. If

74

you sincerely love to write, then the creation of books is not a chore. On the other hand, if you only want the accolades that come from having written a book, then creating said book becomes a daunting task.

The outcome of sincere effort is often quality output, and quality is inspirational in all of its forms. It's inspirational because there is little of it in today's cheaply and quickly manufactured modern world. It's the reason the Steve Jobses of the world stand out. A commitment to quality despite the modern ethos.

Sincerity is a prerequisite to quality, and much like flow states, the more often we are sincere in word and deed, the more often we will come to the condition of sincerity naturally—a condition other people can sense and are attracted to. This is why Tsunetomo wrote, "A samurai should not, in the slightest degree, say or do something faintheartedly. Never forget this. The depth of one's heart is discernible even through something seemingly inconsequential."

On the contrary, when you act insincerely, this too becomes a pattern of behavior. For a samurai insincerity is unacceptable because it leads to impurity in thought and deed. Our actions are like an arch that stretches across our entire life and reveals the depth of our character to those around us (and to future generations). The smallest actions are representative of the whole.

10

CORRECT CONDUCT

"Everything you say or do, every word you write, every
implement you manage, manifests the totality that is
there ... The Way lies in each aspect of your everyday
conduct and activity."

— *Yamaga Soko*

Above all a samurai lives with intention. Knowing how
precious each moment is, none are wasted. He lives knowing
he may die at any time, so there must be a congruence of
thought, word, and deed. This congruence leads to internal
harmony, and when there is internal harmony, all actions are
done with the same balanced spirit.

This is what Takuan Soho meant when he wrote, "Like
a plumb line, anything done at all will be right-mindedness.
This absolutely straight thing is the substance of right-
mindedness and in using the straightness in that core of
the mind as a plumb line, everything produced will exhibit
right-mindedness."

Right-mindedness produces right action. Right action (correct conduct) is the purposeful and directed action taken by a cultivated mind that has undergone introspection and brutal self-analysis, not in one domain but in all.

Honor is a natural extension of correct conduct. Honor is simply the pride we take in our actions. When someone says you acted honorably, they mean you acted correctly, often under difficult circumstances. Acting correctly so that we can take pride in our behavior should always be our goal, especially under duress.

Honor is our barometer for correct conduct. If we are proud of ourselves, then we are proud of the totality of our actions. If we are proud of the totality of our actions, it means that there is no internal conflict in our moment-to-moment existence. This lack of conflict allows us to silence our internal narrative and clears the way for instances of immersion.

Maintaining the harmony we feel when we take right action and the peace of mind this brings us is our ultimate aim, to pacify our monkey mind and instead be governed by our ideal self.

In order for our better nature to reign, however, we must take a macro-level view of our behavior and ask ourselves in every situation how our ideal self would behave and then act accordingly. This takes intention. We must intentionally guide our actions rather than letting instincts blindly pilot us. Using honor as our barometer for correct conduct, we must master the space between impression and reaction and in that scope of time deliberately decide how to act. Legacy is in every word and every deed.

To a samurai, honor was everything. So much so that they were willing to kill and die to protect it. In a terrestrial sense, a warrior's honor and reputation (on and off the battlefield) often equated to land and power. In a higher sense, honor and the accompanying lack of conflict gave a warrior internal harmony. In a complex environment where fortunes could shift rapidly, internal harmony became not just a barometer for correct conduct but an inner sanctum for a warrior to retreat into in the midst of trying circumstances.

Trying circumstances meant samurai understood the fickleness of fortune well. A fragmented and complex political environment created a constant power struggle with a rotating cast of victors, which led to many clans and individual samurai falling in and out of power. This made empathy an extremely practical reality as victorious samurai could see themselves in their defeated opponents. Even the (seemingly gruesome and barbaric) ritual of ceremonially taking and displaying opponents' heads was done with reverence and respect for the fallen foe.

11

EMPATHY

Dealing admirably with others is simply a matter of having empathy, of remembering where we started and how difficult our journey has been and how difficult theirs must be too. It is the very real acknowledgment that with just a few twists of fate we could have easily become that person we scorn. If we had been born to different parents, in a different country or under a different set of circumstances, we could have been an entirely different person. Perhaps one we wouldn't like very much.

When viewed from this perspective, harboring animosity seems senseless. Recognizing that we too could have become that person if the die had been cast differently makes feelings of hostility fall away. Their mistakes could easily be our mistakes. This what Tsunetomo was touching upon when he wrote, "Discrimination, harboring animosity, and causing others to feel estranged is born of a lack of compassion."

We resent those whom we perceive to be malicious, ignorant, lazy, arrogant, and so on. This is because we recognize that capacity for negativity and self-destructiveness in ourselves and hate what we see. As the author Robert M. Pirsig put it, "We always condemn most in others that which we most fear in ourselves."

Next time we feel that sense of resentment toward someone else, we must recognize that same capacity in ourselves. We must attribute those feelings of animosity to fear. We are subconsciously afraid (and consequently angry) that we too harbor those same negative tendencies and that subject to the right set of circumstances, we may also be engaging in the same behavior that we so revile.

Recognition of the fickleness of fortune and appreciation for the difficulty of life are the seeds

of empathy and compassion. This recognition results naturally from a correct perspective that is the product of a cultivated mind.

There are opportunistic reasons for empathy as well. We cannot advance our station in life without the help of others. By being sincere and empathetic we open ourselves up to the good graces of others, and inevitably opportunities will come our way as by-products of the relationships we build.

Building relationships outside of the immediate family (or pack) is a distinctively human trait that springs from empathy and leads to the kindred cooperation we are (sometimes) able to achieve.

As Tsunetomo wrote, "We are kindred members of our domain, a big family, from the day we are born, to the day we die. Can such indomitable trust be found elsewhere?"

The human experience is both a unique and shared phenomenon. As a species (perhaps instinctively) we are moving ever closer to collective consciousness. Technology continues to dismantle the barriers that have typically separated us. Private industry creates ever-advanced forms of communication that shred traditional notions of privacy, and consumers consume voraciously.

We want to share the colorful moments of our lives with others because doing so is distinctly human. Seeking connection is evolutionarily ingrained into the fabric of our being. We want to connect with others, make them feel good, and, in turn, feel good ourselves. Technology is a tool for, and a natural extension of, seeking connection.

As individuals we need to harness the emotional power of connection intentionally. We must make others feel good by paying full attention, being present, and removing thoughts of self. Doing this will raise our stock with others, but more importantly it will raise our stock with ourselves, because the more often we put ourselves in a state of sincere presence, the more we will arrive at this state naturally. The more we arrive at this state naturally, the better our lives become.

When in a state of sincere presence, we act as the silent observer of situations and peer into the hidden mechanisms at work, illuminating the obscured. This includes conversation. When we are present, when we listen with the intent of understanding rather than waiting for our turn to speak, our interactions take on new depth.

On the other hand, when we listen shallowly and our internal narrative dominates the conversation, we muddle the message. We should let our actions, not words, serve as an example for others. Words complicate interaction. Advice, though given with good intentions, often has the tendency to sting more than to heal.

12

BREVITY

"A man's true mind can be known through a single word."
— *Yamamoto Tsunetomo*

The more we speak, the more complexity we visit on a subject. Complexity, though sometimes necessary, is often not. When the object of our speech is to accomplish a tangible goal, such as closing a business deal, the more we say, the worse our position becomes, because when we say more than necessary, we create side roads, paths that takes us everywhere but our intended destination. This becomes especially true (as do most of the principles in this book) during times of struggle and stress.

The impulse to react to events emotionally and neglect the space between impression and reaction is (yet again) rooted in ego. We feel challenged, our ego feels threatened, and emotions take hold. Rather than sticking to our mission and guiding the conversation toward our intended destination, we create an enormous detour with a new mission in mind, defending our bruised sense of self-worth.

On the other hand, reducing complexity (saying as little as necessary) carves a singular path toward our target destination. By speaking with specificity, we reduce complexity. Flowery language leaves room for confusion. Deep thoughts can be conveyed simply. The art of communicating effectively lies in the process of reduction. Use fewer words to say more. As presence increases, reduction becomes easier.

The narrative in our heads becomes less audible over time as we subject it to the harshness of discipline. This makes it easier to listen to others and choose our words with intention. We ought to speak less and listen more. In doing so, mission-critical information will reveal itself to us in the subtleties of conversation.

Before we speak, we should ask ourselves, does what I am about to say get me closer or further away from where I want to guide this conversation? Am I acting intentionally or simply reacting?

Saying only what is necessary at a particular moment in time requires us to have a finely tuned perception that we develop as a product of our daily efforts. Our daily efforts, in turn, reveal themselves to others through our actions and our character.

What we say and what we do, word and deed, must always be in alignment. It is from this place of internal alignment that all harmony flows. This harmony need not be forced upon others. Words will not suffice. Live your truth and let others bear witness. As Tsunetomo wrote, "There is no need to reveal all that is on your mind. Your qualities will be apparent through your daily actions."

13

ACTIONS NOT WORDS

"Learning is the gate that approaches the way, passing through this gate you arrive at the way. But learning is the gate not the house ... Do not read written works and think this is the way, written works are only the gate."
— *Yagyū Munenori*

Your purpose will not be realized through words, only actions. Reading this book and thoroughly understanding the principles contained within is not enough. It's a start, a way to find your path, like guiding markers on the side of the road, but it is not the road. The road must be walked, not read.

This is what Munenori meant when wrote, "If you merely read this book you will not reach the Way of strategy. Absorb the things written in this book. Do not just read, memorize, or imitate, but so that you realize the principle from within your own heart study hard to absorb these things into your body."

Realizing the principle in your own heart means walking a true path in your own life. It means taking these principles and molding them to suit your circumstances and then ruthlessly applying them, over and over, especially when faced with adversity.

I could feel the components that created harmony in my life before I could articulate them. So I dissected that mental state, seeking to replicate it in other areas of my life, and, in doing so, I was able to define the circumstances that created it. Once defined, I was able to accelerate my personal evolution by optimizing my behavior in accordance with the principles that enabled these circumstances.

It's the combination of exploration, discovery, and (most importantly) application of principles that leads to growth. Yet few of us ever make it out of the discovery phase because changing our behavior is hard and most people shun adversity. But difficulty and struggle are necessary conditions for the flowering of the soul. Like a seed in dirt, excellence has no other home. The polarity of the dimension in which we exist requires suffering and excellence to have their silent pact.

14

Dealing With Difficulty And Overcoming Adversity

"A competent man, or one engrossed in a pursuit
he enjoys, will relish the challenge of surmounting
difficulties. There is a huge difference between these
men, and those who feel as though they are drowning
when the going gets tough."
—Yamamoto Tsunetomo

Once we have articulated our purpose, we come to realize that fulfilling that purpose will be a series of continuous challenges, increasing in difficulty, until the end of our lives. Rather than resolve ourselves to it, we embrace it and are thankful that we are able to walk our true path, mindful of the fact that most people will spend an unfulfilled lifetime not walking theirs. The cost of meaning, purpose, and fulfillment is struggle. There is no other way. There is only the way.

We honor our journey by being grateful for the lessons that adversity teaches us. When we complain, we dishonor the journey, shun the lesson, and suffer without reason. Complaining negatively skews our perspective and blinds us to our blessings.

This negative perspective carves a canyon through our mind (much like anxiety) that other thoughts inevitably fall into. It becomes a mired lens through which we begin to see the world. Complaining makes us the center of our thoughts instead of the mission, thus pushing the object of our action further away. The sadness that follows this dissatisfaction is called self-pity, and nothing is more egregious to a samurai than self-pity.

Self-pity is often followed by misdirected anger. We look for (and find) other people or external factors to blame for our misery. Anger of any kind is another behavioral trap that widens the thought canyon and saps our energy. It is a poisonous pattern of thought that corrodes our peace of mind.

Anger is insidious in nature because it's poison that feels like fuel. Although anger may feel like fuel because it motivates action, it clouds judgment, thereby motivating us to take the wrong actions, or motivating us to take the right actions for the wrong reasons.

The problem with doing the right things for the wrong reasons is that eventually we stop doing them, we run out of fuel. Anger is not a sustainable emotion. No one can stay angry for a lifetime. Anger is akin to running on jet fuel while the imperturbable mind feeds on solar power.

Jet fuel allows us to cover short distances quickly (assuming it doesn't blow us up in the process) but requires constant refueling, and its combustive nature corrodes quickly. Solar power, on the other hand, is a renewable source of energy that is in constant supply. It is in tune with the natural order of things, and we can draw from it, at will, for the rest of our lives.

Curb anger and dissatisfaction by exercising gratitude. We often overlook the many things we have to be grateful for, and we forget how trying circumstances can become. We should remind ourselves daily of the multitude of blessings we already have in our life and imagine that complaining pushes those things further away. As if an omnipotent universe heard our grievances as a parent hears those of a spoiled child.

This simple switch in perspective made monumental changes in my life. Prior to pursuing my true purpose, adversity seemed impossible to overcome. Constant complaining made me focus on the seemingly insurmountable obstacles blocking my ascent instead of looking for alternative routes to the summit. This mired lens framed the way I viewed the world because all I could see were hurdles, the sum total of which became impossible to overcome.

The pursuit of my true purpose turned obstacles into opportunities for immersion. I was, as Tsunetomo wrote, engrossed in a pursuit I enjoyed and relishing the challenge of overcoming difficulty. The act of which became its own reward.

This is not to say that I have rid myself of this mindset altogether. My mind is not imperturbable, and difficult circumstances will sometimes cause me to voice my dissatisfaction. But when I do, I recognize the complaining (and dissatisfaction in general) for what it is—ego's distorted narration driven by expectations I was foolish enough to let manifest in my mind.

Rather than identify with disappointment, I distance myself from the initial thought before it becomes a pattern of thinking by simply labeling what I'm feeling, and doing so causes that emotion to subside. This process, much like meditation, silences the ego's narration and creates the distance needed for the effective analysis that leads to correct conduct.

When we avoid the behavioral traps of the ego, we achieve presence, and presence gives us access to deep insight that makes seemingly ordinary moments extraordinary. Buddhists call this the miracle of the ordinary. Ordinary moments are what color life. We must not overlook the beauty of life because we are focused solely on our mission. We must enjoy the scenery on our journey of transcendence if we are to transcend at all.

Our evolution requires presence and presence requires us to be engaged in the here and now. In doing so, the miraculous quality of ordinary moments becomes apparent to us. Noticing this causes us to have gratitude, and someone who is grateful cannot complain in the same breath.

During difficult times we should look back to before our journey began, to when we were still lost and had not yet found our way. We should think of ourselves as a traveler lost in the desert, who after untold time of aimless wandering has finally found a road back to salvation. Though we know not what difficulties may lie ahead, or how long this road may be, we know with certainty that it is our path—the road that takes us to where we need to go.

All we have to do is churn gravel under our feet, one step at a time, with purpose and intention, remembering to enjoy the scenery along the way, and when the inevitable thunderstorm hits, we take comfort in having found our true path and are indifferent to getting wet. Churning gravel under our feet is called discipline.

15
DISCIPLINE

Discipline is the grindstone upon which we sharpen our mind-sword. It is the repetitive efforts we take day in and day out to become our ideal self. The more sincere we are in our efforts, the greater the reward. As Takuan Soho wrote, "The enlightening of one's mind depends on the depths of one's efforts."

Discipline amounts to smart and consistent effort directed toward a specific goal that, once actualized, inevitably impacts all areas of our life. Much like immersive experience, once discipline takes hold in one domain, it begins to bleed into others. We all crave internal harmony. Discipline will often provide that harmony in one area of our life. We work hard at something and get better at it, which feels good, so we do more of it.

After enough repetition, this cycle becomes ingrained in us and discipline begins to seep into other areas of our life, thus creating a self-perpetuating cycle that fuels immersive experience; and as we have already learned, immersive experiences when properly directed become the building blocks for a fulfilling life.

We should seek discipline. This may involve finding an external discipline that is both challenging and enjoyable. An external discipline is any activity that is challenging, has objective measurements of improvement, and is typically done with or against other people. This includes yoga, competitive sports of any kind, martial arts, memory competitions, and weightlifting, among others. Discipline comes in many forms.

An internal discipline is a singular pursuit (like the creation of this book) that we pursue in isolation. Internal disciplines are often more difficult to master than external disciplines because we are not publicly accountable. Begin with an external discipline. Work at getting better at something in the light of day, where other people can see your progress. Once the process of improvement becomes second nature, apply this methodology to your singular pursuits. Reality is malleable, and discipline is both the hammer and chisel with which we carve our masterpiece.

Practicing an external discipline (jujitsu) gave me the tools I needed to accomplish an internal discipline (writing). I applied the lessons I learned on the mats to other areas of my life, and the result (among others) was the creation of this book, the sense of purpose this gave me, and the profound change that had on my character.

If you have not yet found an external discipline to pursue, consider jujitsu. I firmly believe that every person (especially children) should learn jujitsu. It is the single best training ground for actualizing human potential and (unlike other martial arts) provides objective measures of progress.

Jujitsu (in its original form) was one of the cornerstones of a samurai's training regimen, along with archery, horsemanship, swordsmanship, and calligraphy. Jujitsu was a grappling discipline that (when executed effectively) enabled lightly armored samurai to subdue a heavily armored (and consequently less mobile) opponent using leverage and technique instead of force.

In the twentieth century, Japanese Jujitsu was refined by *Kanō Jigorō* to be more effective in a modern setting. This new style fit the more practical realities of life in industrialized twentieth-century Japan, where combat between two armed and armored opponents was highly unlikely, and instead adapted itself to the far more likely possibility of combat between unarmed opponents in the ever-denser urban centers of modern Japan.

Jigorō's new jujitsu variation stopped using weapons and put an emphasis on throws, sweeps, joint locks, and chokes. Instead of armor, his students would wear a gi, an item of clothing that is similar to a suit or coat someone might wear on the street, which made *Jigorō*'s new techniques extremely effective in real-life combat scenarios. This new discipline became judo.

One of Jigorō's disciples, Mitsuyo Maeda, traveled to Brazil in 1917 where he taught judo to Helio Gracie and his brothers Carlos and George. The Gracies would go on to further adapt and refine judo to work effectively in street fights. Their style, which focused more on ground control, while still incorporating judo's throws, sweeps, joint locks, and chokes, became Brazilian Jujitsu.

Brazilian Jujitsu would go on to dominate the new sport of Mixed Martial Arts (MMA) later that century. Royce Gracie (Helio's grandson) fought in and won the first internationally televised MMA tournament (UFC 1) against much larger opponents who were equally skilled in other disciplines. It was here that the world first got a glimpse of the ruthless efficiency of the gentle art of jujitsu.

MMA has evolved and for the most part is no longer dominated by specialists. The majority of professional fighters have a large toolkit of skills from various grappling and striking disciplines in their arsenal. It has become necessary to learn a myriad of different techniques to be able to compete in MMA today.

Consequently, I don't think people should learn jujitsu purely for self-defense. Rather, jujitsu should be practiced for the strength it cultivates in both our mind and body and the transformation this has on our character. Jujitsu is an ancient practice inherited directly from the samurai of old that teaches us, in real time, life lessons that we might not otherwise learn.

These lessons (discussed throughout this book) encapsulate the samurai spirit in the modern era, and as we improve in jujitsu, we internalize the improvement process and absorb the samurai spirit, which strengthens our mind and creates confidence in our own agency, and this teaches us that anything can be accomplished with smart and consistent effort. Consistent effort is (for the most part) self-explanatory, and the ideal formula for creating consistent effort will be detailed later in this chapter. But what is a smart effort, and how can we quantify it?

The famous business strategist Peter Drucker once wrote that what gets measured, gets managed, and what gets managed, improves. This maxim is also applicable to our life. Consistent effort is good; smart and consistent effort is best. Smart effort requires us to measure things, judge our progress, and concentrate our efforts in areas that require more of our focus.

This practice is not domain dependent. In the physical domain, it can mean finding a workout routine and diet, setting tangible goals and measuring progress by writing down workouts, counting calories, and recording weight or body composition. If you're practicing a sport (like jujitsu), this can mean objectively analyzing your performance and deliberately improving your shortcomings.

In the personal domain it can mean having daily routines of reflection and intention (perhaps journaling and meditation) that allow us to envision our ideal selves and measure progress toward that internal harmony.

In the professional domain this can mean setting career goals (objectives) and having clearly defined metrics (what the author and entrepreneur John Doerr calls key results) that indicate progress toward those goals. Consistent effort, measured progress, objective analysis, readjustment, and further effort form a cycle of improvement that can be applied to any of life's arenas. This cycle is how we forge the sharpest version of ourselves and get better at the things that matter.

As Munenori puts it, "When potential is not mature, function will not be manifested. Potential will mature and great function will issue forth if you continually maintain awareness and accumulate effort in all your disciplines. If potential coagulates or becomes set, there will be no function."

He reminds us that without accumulated effort, the things we hope for never come to pass. Function will not be manifested, and potential will coagulate. If we wish to avoid a paralysis of our potential, then we must embrace consistent effort—not for a season as we strive for a specific goal, but rather for a lifetime as we strive for all of our goals.

The optimal formula for consistent effort is what author Jim Collins calls the 20-mile march. The 20-mile march sets both a lower boundary and an upper boundary, a hurdle that we jump over and a ceiling that we will not rise above. It requires both the ambition to achieve and the self-control to hold back. The 20-mile march forces us to be consistent in our efforts while ensuring that we don't burn out, thus getting us to our target destination faster than we would otherwise arrive. Speed via regimentation. Collins described it like this:

Imagine you're standing with your feet in the Pacific Ocean in San Diego, California, looking inland. You're about to embark on a three-thousand-mile walk, from San Diego to the tip of Maine. On the first day, you march 20 miles, making it out of town. On the second day, you march 20 miles. And again, on the third day, you march 20 miles, heading into the heat of the desert. It's hot, more than a hundred degrees, and you want to rest in the cool of your tent. But you don't. You get up and you march 20 miles. You keep the pace, 20 miles a day. Then the weather cools, and you're in comfortable conditions with the wind at your back, and you could go much farther. But you hold back, modulating your effort. You stick with your 20 miles. Then you reach the Colorado high mountains and get hit by snow, wind, and temperatures below zero—and all you want to do is stay in your tent. But you get up. You get dressed. You march your 20 miles. You keep up the effort—20 miles, 20 miles, 20 miles—then you cross into the plains, and it's glorious springtime, and you can go 40 or 50 miles in a day. But you don't. You sustain your pace, marching 20 miles. And eventually, you get to Maine. Now, imagine another person who starts out with you on the same day in San Diego. He gets all excited by the journey and logs 40 miles the first day. Exhausted from his first gigantic day, he wakes up to hundred-degree temperatures. He decides to hang out until the weather cools, thinking, "I'll make it up when conditions improve." He maintains this pattern—big days with good conditions, whining and waiting in his tent on bad days—as he moves across the western United States. Just before the Colorado high mountains, he gets a spate of great weather and he goes all out, logging 40- to 50-mile days to make up lost ground. But then he hits a huge winter storm when utterly exhausted. It nearly kills him and he hunkers down in his tent, waiting for spring. When spring finally comes, he emerges, weakened, and stumbles off toward Maine. By the time he enters Kansas City, you, with your relentless 20-mile march, have already reached the tip of Maine. You win, by a huge margin.

The 20-mile march brought this book into existence. I used this methodology to complete the book you're reading while working full-time and training seven days a week. (It's amazing how much time we have when we cut out the superfluous.)

The execution was simple. Every weekday from 5:00 to 9:00 a.m., my phone on silent, cup of coffee by my side, Schubert, Mahler, or Beethoven playing softly in the background, I'd sit down and write, undistracted, until the session was at an end.

It didn't matter how I felt or what seemingly pressing responsibilities I had to take care of that day. Writing came first. This consistency built up over time and is now a lifelong routine. My mornings are, and forever will be, reserved for writing.

This gives me peace of mind because I know I can maintain this output, thereby giving me a sustainable creative outlet for the rest of my life. This is in complete contrast to my formerly wild and unsustainable creative output, consisting of long sprints as I attempted to finish work in time for a deadline. The act of which causes stress and takes the very thing I'm seeking (the immersion that leads to tranquility) out of the creative process.

In the end, the steady and consistent 20-mile march methodology took me further, much faster than I would have otherwise been able to go.

The key factor to the change in my creative process was, yet again, a switch in perspective from the micro to the macro. Writing, I realized, was not about the individual work I was producing in the short term, but rather the body of work I would be able to produce over the course of my lifetime. With this realization writing became a marathon, not a sprint, and my method of production shifted from erratic output to the regimented and (consequently) sustainable creative output that leads to lasting sanity.

Whichever path we choose, it will be a long-term commitment, and our goal, through the pursuit of that purpose, is to improve incrementally, in every area of our life, for the rest of our life. This lifelong commitment to continual improvement is a cornerstone of the samurai's ethos and arrives at the heart of what it means to be a samurai in any era.

16

Kaizen (Continual Improvement)

"Make no provision for retreat. This means to have
a mind that will not be altered. It means that a man
should be mindful that, although he advances well
once or twice, he should not retreat when he is tired or
in unusual circumstances."

—*Takuan Soho*

We are not on a war campaign for a season but for all
seasons. Our battle never ends. Victory is a door not
a destination. Subjecting ourselves (and our actions) to
objective analysis and taking disciplined action to remedy
the faults that our objective analysis uncovers is the process
we must repeat over the course of a lifetime to become the
person we want to be.

The person we aspire to become is not static but, like all
things in the universe, an ever-evolving, interconnected part

of a greater whole that progresses in harmony until the exterior shell expires, leaving the contents of the interior (memories, works, and soul) to eternity. By honoring this process of ascension, we find freedom and ultimately happiness.

Always striving to be a better person, continually seeking to increase harmony, and making incremental improvements over the course of a lifetime are the foundational pillars of kaizen. This process requires us to have the humility to see our faults as well as the drive and discipline to defeat them.

Unlike (some) modern MMA fighters, samurai of old recognized that improvement (and consequently excellence) necessitates and is preceded by humility. If lifelong excellence is our aim, then maintaining humility throughout the course of our lives is an essential factor in achieving it.

We can see this mindset reflected in the writing of Tsunetomo. When discussing his achievements, he wrote, "I do not know how to defeat others. All I know is the path to defeat myself. Today one must be better than yesterday, and tomorrow better than today. The pursuit of excellence is a lifelong quest that has no end."

Defeating others is fuel for our ego; defeating ourselves is its death. To surmount obstacles, we must first surmount ourselves. The continual improvement that leads to mastery of self is simply a lifelong individual competition. We are in a competition with ourselves, always striving to be a better person than we were the day before, for the rest of our lives. When we regularly tackle our own shortcomings, we also begin to conquer life's many hurdles as a by-product of our efforts.

This is what Musashi meant when he wrote, "Study strategy over the years and achieve the spirit of the warrior. Today is victory over yourself of yesterday; tomorrow is your victory over lesser men."

To achieve the spirit of a warrior, we must override our impulses, control our emotions, and intentionally guide our actions. By doing this we overcome our biological programing and defeat our lesser selves. This leads to a state of imperturbability from which all other obstacles become surmountable. In defeating our demons, we acquire the toolset needed to surmount the external obstacles blocking our path as well. Thus, through the defeat of the self we are victorious.

However, we must not let our victories blind us. Yes, we should enjoy them, but like all things in life, we must let them go. If we relish our victories too long, we stop working on improvement, and the way, our path, requires us to churn gravel beneath our feet, to walk on, lest we are lost.

Being lost is akin to spiritual death. A slow roasting of our soul. We've felt it before and hope to never feel it again. Thus, to avoid this fate, we must strive for consistent improvement and have a method in place to examine our actions, discover our faults, and take corrective action. As Tsunetomo wrote, "Knowing the Way is to know your own faults. Discovering your imperfections with endless introspection and to remedy them by spending your life training body and mind (shugyō)."

Tsunetomo reminds us that whichever method of improvement we choose, it must be a regularly occurring affair for the rest of our lives. As circumstances are always in flux, we need to ask ourselves a high volume of questions on a regular basis to form the opinions necessary to act correctly. This mental exercise leaves us well prepared for life's hurdles. This is what Tsunetomo was touching upon he wrote, "A man can achieve much as long as he prepares himself daily."

Preparation equates to having regular routines of reflection and corrective action that become ingrained in us. A systematic process, to which we instinctively subject all things in our life. Nothing is off-limits. No layer is too deep, and no island is too far.

"Any man who wants to master the essence of my strategy must research diligently, training morning and evening. Thus he can polish his skill, become free from self, and realize extraordinary ability," said Miyamoto Musashi.

The process Musashi described amounts to achieving technical mastery over a specific domain, the act of which leads to the dissolution of our ego and, consequently, the elevation of our mind. Imagine a martial artist who masters their discipline and, in doing so, adopts a mindset and creates a framework to which they can subject all other things in their life. They have a process by which they can examine reality, filter out the superfluous, and, as a result, generate internal harmony.

When we sincerely search for our true path, we inevitably find what we are looking for, and our daily efforts in the pursuit of that purpose bring us harmony and clarity, which give us a framework to make big decisions in the other areas of our life. This is what Tsunetomo meant when he wrote, "Important matters are few in number and can be studied carefully in the course of daily affairs."

Individual decisions are simply a singular application of the larger questions we have already answered. All things boil down to congruence. All we have to ask ourselves is this: Is this action congruent with the person I want to be? Does it get me closer to where I want to go, personally, professionally, or spiritually?

If we are devoid of fear, unperturbed by defeat, and have a clear understanding of our purpose, then even the heaviest of decisions can be made with alacrity and clarity. We can truly, as Tsunetomo wrote, "think lightly when deciding on weighty matters."

Tsunetomo expanded on this idea when he wrote, "The prepared warrior is not only able to solve problems in a quick and commendable fashion by virtue of his life experience, but he can react appropriately through his comprehension of measures to meet any scenario. He is always ready … Decisions will be difficult to make when one's heart is adrift. With an unperturbed, invigorated, and dignified state of mind, resolutions can be made within seven breaths."

Deciding within the space of seven breaths requires a level of self-understanding and self-control that can only be achieved after years of practicing kaizen. With enough practice, long-term practitioners of kaizen achieve a level of self-mastery that seems ethereal to the rest of us. From this place, situations can be read clearly, reacted to quickly, and dealt with effectively.

Observing someone in this mental state is like watching a grandmaster play chess—each move comes as a natural extension of the next. Masters play as if inspired from a higher plane, and though their mind is in motion, they themselves are immovable, impervious to circumstance and indifferent to fate.

This mentality gives its owner the ability to recognize, create, and seize opportunities where their competitors see none. This ability is the by-product of an imperturbable mind. Recognizing and seizing opportunities becomes easier as we move toward this state.

17
OPPORTUNITIES

By striving for excellence in our chosen field we reach a state of mental imperturbability which, after enough time and practice, becomes our mind's default mode. Consequently, as we move toward mastery in our chosen field, we begin to recognize opportunities we never saw, in places we never thought to look.

Seizing these opportunities, however, is far more difficult in practice than in theory. The reason, once again, is fear. Procrastination and indecision are forms of fear that paralyze action, and if we are paralyzed, we cannot pursue our purpose and instead are confined to the prison of an unfulfilled life.

Actions lead to outcomes; inaction leads to none. We can find numerous examples of an underdog, a dark horse, beating out the competition by taking quick and effective action when their larger and more entrenched competitors lagged or took none.

Case in point: Netflix, the scrappy bootstrapped start-up that made the corporate behemoth Blockbuster's business model obsolete. Blockbuster didn't recognize the value of shipping (and ultimately streaming) content to customers. A missed opportunity that literally cost them their business.

In business as in life, the prize frequently goes to those who strike first and strike often. Size pales in comparison to speed, intensity, and persistence. As Hirayama Heigen once wrote, "A ferocious tiger that hesitates does not compare to a stinging bee or scorpion."

Heigen was right. Those of us who would pose for a picture with a sedated lion would flee in terror at the sight (or sound) of an angry hornet. But why do we fear the hornet's sting more than the lion's bite, despite the consequences being far less dire? Because we know the hornet is serious, committed to doing us harm at any cost. Commitment and ferocity of deployment toward a goal make the achievement of that goal far more likely.

Large entrenched institutions tend to move slower than their smaller counterparts. Smaller organizations that survive learn how to use mobility to their advantage. This is true in warfare, where guerilla fighters attack larger forces swiftly and by surprise, fleeing before absorbing heavy causalities of their own, and it's true in business as well, where young scrappy start-ups like Uber disrupt traditional industries at breakneck speeds before regulators and competitors can mobilize.

We must implement this principle in our own life too. Once we recognize an opportunity and decide to take action, it is crucial that we do so swiftly, with full focus and commitment. Tsunetomo articulated this principle well. He wrote, "Good opportunities will present themselves to those who show patience. All that is required is forbearance, and when the right moment comes, act swiftly without slackening."

Through training, fear gives way to focus. Focus allows us to identify opportunities, and discipline allows us to seize them through action. Once we have decided that an action is congruent with our mission, we must plan and execute that action with immediacy. The tasks we let linger seldom get done. As Tsunetomo noted, "Something that is not done at that time and at that place will remain unfinished for a lifetime."

Once we have reached a decision based on sound logic but waiver in taking action, we are doing so because of fear. Removing fear (and consequently ourselves) from the equation and just acting is the bridge that takes us from the wilderness to the road.

Tsunetomo explained this principle succinctly. He reminded the reader that "your life will become simple and clear if you are unwavering in purpose, knowing that 'now' is the time to act."

Facing our fear, time and time again, is the only tangible way to change our life. If we don't make frightening choices and put ourselves in uncomfortable situations, we will never improve. But fear often disguises itself as logic and reason, thereby complicating this process.

Sometimes, when we reach a decision, our self-defeating narrative begins to add layers of complexity to each scenario, demanding we examine each possible variable of an obscure future, which is an impossible task and an impediment to action. Once a decision has been made based on sound logic, additional thoughts about that subject will yield negative returns if left unchecked. There is nothing to be gained from excessive contemplation. This is what Tsunetomo meant when he wrote, "One's judgment will diminish with prolonged deliberation."

Thoughts can be a prison. If you ever lie awake at night with a racing mind, you have an inkling of what it's like to be a slave to your mind. To quell the seeds of self-doubt, we need a concrete formula for when and how to take decisive action.

The formula that has worked best for me is a thought exercise created by the author Jim Collins. He describes the process like this:

> Picture yourself at sea, a hostile ship bearing down on you. You have a limited amount of gunpowder. You take all your gunpowder and use it to fire a big cannonball. The cannonball flies out over the ocean … and misses the target, off by 40 degrees. You turn to your stockpile and discover that you're out of gunpowder. You die.

But suppose instead that when you see the ship bearing down, you take a little bit of gunpowder and fire a bullet. It misses by 40 degrees. You make another bullet and fire. It misses by 30 degrees. You make a third bullet and fire, missing by only 10 degrees. The next bullet hits—ping!—the hull of the oncoming ship. Now, you take all the remaining gunpowder and fire a big cannonball along the same line of sight, which sinks the enemy ship. You live.

WHAT MAKES A BULLET?

A bullet is an empirical test aimed at learning what works and that meets three criteria:

1. A bullet is low cost. Note: the size of a bullet grows as the enterprise grows; a cannonball for a $1 million enterprise might be a bullet for a $1 billion enterprise.

2. A bullet is low risk. Note: low risk doesn't mean high probability of success; low risk means that there are minimal consequences if the bullet goes awry or hits nothing.

3. A bullet is low distraction. Note: this means low distraction for the overall enterprise; it might be very high distraction for one or a few individuals.

This formula is applicable in life as much as it is in business. For example, if you'd like to write for a living but are working in another field, rather than just flat-out quit your job, test the waters first. Create content, improve your skills, build an audience, get a feel for how much revenue you could generate from writing, adjust your expenses accordingly, and then commit yourself fully.

This process takes some of the mystery out of an already frightening situation. You're not blindly jumping off a cliff and instead have a measuring stick with which you can test the depth of the water. Musashi aptly compared this process to a ship leaving harbor. He wrote,

> I believe this "crossing at a ford" occurs often in man's lifetime. It means setting sail even though your friends stay in harbor, knowing the route, knowing the soundness of your ship and the favor of the day. When all the conditions are met, and there is perhaps a favorable wind, or a tailwind, then set sail. If the wind changes within a few miles of your destination, you must row across the remaining distance without sail. If you attain this spirit, it applies to everyday life. You must always think of crossing at a ford.

Yet despite our best efforts, not every crossing will be successful. There will be failure, there may in fact be catastrophic failures. As we've already learned, we must accept the inevitability of failure to preserve our sanity and our dignity. Crossing at a ford means taking action despite this inevitability. It means reaching a decision based on sound logic, then quieting the voices of doubt, taking action, and responding to the challenges that arise from a place of self-mastery instead of fear. It requires us to meet each situation fluidly, with a buoyant mind that can adapt as necessary to reach our fixed goal. Obstacles are overcome through emptiness, not by force.

As Munenori wrote, "Action is accomplished with a full insight into all principles, lightly throwing those principles off and letting none remain in the mind. It is accomplished by keeping the mind empty."

It is at this point in the journey, when our crossing at a ford is confronted with catastrophic failure, that we reaffirm what we've always known and have secretly feared. We are not in control. We have moves and countermoves but ultimately life holds the cards. Sometimes, through no fault of our own, the worst comes to pass. In these moments, it is crucial that we hold steadfast to our principles if we hope to preserve our peace of mind. And for tranquility to flourish, we must not only make peace with whatever circumstances life throws at us but learn to love them.

18
LOVING FATE

By learning to love our fate, we fortify our mind against the tyranny of circumstance. Nothing can happen to us against our will if we are prepared for all outcomes. Failure affects us least of all. If we can divorce our mental well-being from outcomes over which we ultimately have no control, then we are impervious to circumstance.

This is the pinnacle of an imperturbable mind. Being disturbed in any capacity means that our mind is not free to move toward an aim of our choosing and instead is stuck, contemplating an object or end that no amount of contemplation or action can change. It is from this fountainhead that all worry springs.

Takuan Soho explained this best. He said, "The mind of attachment arises from the stopping mind. So does the cycle of transmigration. This stopping becomes the bonds of life and death. If the mind does not stop with things, it will not be stained by them."

Our fear, anger, worry, and pain bind us to misery because psychological trauma of any kind is a stopping of the mind. Our mind relives that moment over and over again, pulling us out of the present and away from joy and anchoring us to the past where we can inflict fresh psychological wounds on ourselves daily.

We hold the key to our own bondage and voluntarily wear the shackles of our past pain. We can remove our chains with one word, *acceptance*. The mind that does not stop with things, will not be stained by them. This is true in all of life's many domains.

But how can we move beyond acceptance and learn to not only accept but love our fate? Through a proper perspective that recognizes pain as a sign of growth. In much the same way that weightlifters learn to love the soreness that accompanies a hard workout session because they know what that pain represents: growth. If growth is the goal, then pain is the price.

We don't have to wait until the event is over to learn the lesson that adversity has to teach. We can recognize this value in the midst of difficult circumstances and in doing so our pain turns to pride. Here is a concrete example.

My girlfriend of three years broke up with me on Christmas Eve. Things had been rocky with us for a while, so the breakup wasn't a surprise. What was a surprise was the way things ended. I was in a foreign country by myself, and my mother had passed away less than a month before, so naturally, I was feeling a little low. My then girlfriend and I were supposed to go to her parents' house for dinner that evening, the idea of which brought some welcome warmth into my heart, but she had other plans.

She ignored my messages all day and then got on a train to go see her folks. On the way there she sent me a voice message to let me know that not only had she left without me, but she would be moving on without me. There had been no fight that precipitated this, no infidelity, no argument, just a sudden goodbye. When I read that final message, my initial reaction was self-pity followed by misplaced anger, but that feeling was quickly replaced by relief and then pride, because I recognized, in the moment, the value of the gift she had just given me.

I thought of the frustration that comes from unrequited love and the countless future arguments we would have had as a result. I thought of the resentment that people feel toward each other when they are in a relationship that has passed its expiration date and the slow callousness that brings to their soul.

She had just spared me years of that torture. Sure, her timing was terrible, but her heart was in the right place. By pushing through the pain of my initial knee-jerk reaction, I was able to see the situation clearly and immediately learn the lesson that adversity had to teach. In doing so my pain became a source of pride because I recognized it as a sign of my growth.

I learned this skill the hard way. A year prior to this I went through the worst financial crisis of my personal and professional life. I was running a company that went from being successful to not producing any income seemingly overnight.

I was worse than ill prepared for this. I had almost no savings and heavy overhead. Whatever the opposite of bootstrapped is, that's what I was. My penthouse became a prison. Not only could I not pay the rent, but I couldn't afford to fix the basic things that would break around the house. Then things went from bad to worse. Rather than close up shop and admit to myself that this crossing at a ford had ended with a sunken ship, I tried to row on.

I drove myself deeper into poverty and consequently deeper into despair. I was less than penniless; I had no income, my bank accounts were overdrawn, and I was living on borrowed money from friends and family. This caused a crisis of confidence, and self-doubt became the staple of my internal narrative.

When I finally ran out of options, I was left with only acceptance. I had to accept the terrible circumstance as reality. The business had failed, and it was time to move on. So I did, and pulled myself out of the hole I'd dug by getting a job doing what I should have been doing all along, writing (and to some extent marketing). It paid a lot less than I was used to making, but the act of writing filled me with meaning and gave me a sense of purpose.

There was another ancillary benefit to this seemingly adverse situation and that was extreme fiscal responsibility. Before my personal financial crisis, I had been extremely fiscally irresponsible. I would make money and spend almost all of it on things that I didn't need, things that brought me no real joy. Now, out of necessity, I became extremely fiscally responsible. I tracked every dollar I spent, cut out the superfluous, and learned to live far beneath my means.

If I had continued being successful in what author Steven Pressfield calls a shadow career, I never would have quit and consequently would have spent an unfulfilled lifetime chasing shiny objects of prestige, hollow though they are. Similarly, if I hadn't been forced to live beneath my means, I never would have done so on my own.

Now my work brings me fulfillment and my finances give me peace of mind. Knowing that I can easily pay for my expenses with just a fraction of my income creates a calmness that permeates all things. Simplicity and the art of reduction work not only in speech but in our lives too.

It was only later that I would realize the massive, life-changing benefits that adversity had gifted me. I spent months in a dark miserable place without reason. A prisoner to my thoughts and a slave to my fears. It was the most unhappy I have ever been in my adult life. All for nothing. If I could only have fast-forwarded a year down the road, I would have seen what a gift this circumstance truly was.

It was during this time that I started doing jujitsu, discovered martial philosophy, and began to apply these principles to my life. As my perspective changed, so did my reality. When the changes became tangible and I was able to reflect on my former folly, I realized how foolish it was to let my emotions consume the moment and muddle the lesson. I would never let myself be that miserable again.

Because of this experience I was well prepared for the breakup. When I felt the initial rush of self-pity and anger, I immediately recognized it for what it was, a stopping of the mind, which stains the mind. Labeling what I was feeling created the distance needed to extract the lesson from this particular circumstance as it was occurring. My ability to overcome my initial emotional reaction was a sign of my growth and this filled me with pride.

Pain is an opportunity for growth, though this may be difficult to see and accept in the midst of it. We must lean into pain if we hope to learn from it. Every time we feel bad, there is a lesson to be learned, and if we seek to profit from our pain, we first need to find the source of our discontent. Once we have identified the source of incongruence, we must take corrective action. Usually that action takes the form of self-improvement, since the seed of our misery is most often ourselves.

Pain turns to suffering when we prolong it with thoughts. If there is nothing to deliberate about, let thoughts go. Excessive thinking causes us to miss opportunities for joy.

Thinking does us no good if the outcome of those thoughts is misery and paralysis.

I am writing this book with full awareness of its potential failure. I have accepted failure as an inevitable part of my path and have chosen to proceed in spite of it. I accept that this book may not sell well, and that people may if fact hate it, yet I give these thoughts no space in my mind. I see my path and I am committed to walking it, whatever the external conditions may be.

Why (you may ask) would I proceed in light of this potential failure? Why dedicate so much time and energy to something that may not pan out? Because I love to write and the mental anguish of leaving that ambition unfulfilled far outweighs the fear of rejection and failure.

Preparation and mindset are crucial, but once those have been accounted for and possible outcomes have been weighed and embraced, there is nothing else to deliberate about. Mount horse, hold spear, charge line. All other thoughts are superfluous. We are the stinging hornet, not the sedated lion.

Life is war, and when we're at war, things will happen that won't always be to our liking. Should we abandon the mission then? Call off the assault?

No. Death ends our mission for us. Until then we grind, we seek to impose our will on reality, and when reality imposes circumstances on us that contradict our will, we accept them, and through acceptance learn to love them. We accept defeat, heartbreak, and death as the inevitable consequences of an active and proper life.

Taking action leads to outcomes, not all of which will be favorable; however, the alternative, inaction, paralysis, is a fate worse than death. For unavoidable circumstances that are not the result of actions deliberately taken (like death), acceptance is the only sensible course of action, difficult as it may be.

What comes after death, like all future events, is unknowable, and the mind fears what it doesn't know. Since all future events are essentially unknowable, this groundless fear amounts to a fear of reality itself. And like all forms of fear, we must learn to overcome it if we hope to attain peace of mind, especially in the midst of trying circumstances.

Thus, the imperturbable mind accepts its inevitable transmigration into the unknown without fear, for what could fear change? When we have transcended fear through acceptance and eventually love, we've learned to live in harmony with nature.

19

HARMONY WITH
NATURE

The most difficult circumstances to accept are those imposed on us by nature. We age, our bodies fall apart, and the people we love disappear. All things are in flux, and each day we inch closer to death. Life disappears inch by inch not mile by mile. As Takuan Soho reminded us, "In the end, there is no standing still for either men or things."

Depending on our perspective, this fact can be liberating or debilitating. We too shall disappear, and this can give our lives context and meaning, or it can fill us with dread. How we choose to respond to the inevitability of nature determines how well we are able to live. If we fear the inevitable, we cannot be fully present, engaged, and alive. But if we are able to push through that fear, time and time again, we become indifferent to the inevitability of nature.

We ought not to fear the inevitability of nature, as this is out of our control; instead, we should fear the unlived life.

Death comes for us all, but the unlived life only plagues those who accept their disease. A disease that leaves the body intact but rots our soul. Benjamin Franklin was right, "Most people die at 25 and aren't buried till they're 75."

We die a little each day when we live unfulfilled, and how can we be fulfilled if we have not yet made peace with what we are and where we're going? We forget that we are nature, that we are a part of everything as much as everything is a part of us. We are a unique expression of the universe manifested in this space and time, much like a wave is a unique expression of the ocean.

Picture an individual wave roaring across a rough sea. No other wave will ever have those exact dimensions or be in the same place at the same time ever again. Yet each wave is inseparable from the ocean, and when it's done expressing its uniqueness, it crashes on the shore and is pulled back from whence it came, to be reconstituted, recycled, and, in a sense, born again.

A human being is the same. Part of, and inseparable from, a greater whole. This inseparableness is known to the samurai as nonduality. A Buddhist concept that permeates the warrior's views on life and death.

20

NONDUALITY

"If we observe phenomena closely, it cannot be
thought that anything between heaven and earth is
really different. If we see differences, it is due to the
narrowness of our vision."

— *T a k u a n S o h o*

Our perception is biased. Most of us are dismissive and unaccepting of that which cannot be perceived with our five senses, even when presented with solid evidence that contradicts that perception.

Bacteria are a perfect case in point. When bacteria were first discovered, people (including people in the scientific community) vehemently resisted this new finding and continued to deny its existence. Because the discovery of bacteria challenged conventional wisdom and was beyond the scope of our immediate human perception, it was met with doubt and disdain. Despite this initial resistance, however, bacteria's existence is now a widely recognized fact.

A myriad of other examples follow this same pattern of counterintuitive discovery, vehement opposition, intense investigation, and then general acceptance. Consequently, we must admit that our knowledge and our tools of perception are limited.

As Tsunetomo noted, "It is folly to assume that everything in our mysterious world can be understood by the human mind … There are some things that you gradually come to understand. There are some things that you realize with effort. Then, there are other matters that you will never be able to comprehend at all."

This is not a diminishment of the pursuit of scientific knowledge. On the contrary, it is through this pursuit that we are able to peer into the hidden mechanisms that govern our world and illuminate the unknown. And as a species we have been incredibly successfully at doing this, but as individuals, we must accept that we will never have a complete picture of reality.

There will always be an inseparable element of mystery from our existence. And the greatest mystery of all is life's origin. Not the origin of our species, but rather that of our universe and, consequently, life and consciousness itself. How did an unconscious hunk of matter that burst from nothing give birth to everything?

Three hundred years before Albert Einstein was born, Yamamoto Tsunetomo was able to glean the truth about the nature of our universe through careful observation and contemplation. He expressed the contradictory nature of existence when he wrote, "Our bodies are given life from the midst of nothingness. Existing where there is nothing is the meaning of the phrase, 'Form is emptiness.' That all things are provided for by nothingness is the meaning of the phrase, 'Emptiness is form.' One should not think that these are two separate things."

A cold, dead vacuum that produces life seems contradictory in nature, but the more we learn about the universe, the more contradictions we discover. At a microscopic level the observable universe behaves in shockingly contradictory ways to the laws of general relativity. And that same cold, seemingly dead vacuum produced our planet, which in turn produced us, and we are very much alive. As Seneca, the prolific Stoic philosopher, once wrote, "Eternity consists of opposites."

No one thing in our world is really separate from anything else. We are all just manifestations of the mystery expressing itself in different forms. Like an ocean expressing itself as a wave. But our limited powers of perception prevent us from seeing the ocean.

"As a rule, a thing born cannot be without Form, so we speak of the Essential Quality of Form. Although Form may change in multitudinous ways, as Form it is the same. The ordinary man is unable to see beyond Form," according to Takuan Soho.

Our goal in every domain of life is to see beyond the narrowness of our vision, to expand our perception so that we may peer into the hidden principles that govern our reality. The ordinary man is unable to see beyond form, but we are not ordinary men. We are warriors. We have sharpened our mind-sword and fortified our inner citadel. We understand that form is temporary, but essence is eternal.

The warrior knows the impermanent nature of reality intimately, and this insight guides his actions. Death gives context to life. The warrior lives deeply because he knows that death is ever present. This day could be his last.

Keeping the end in sight makes us focus on the here and now, and though we are focused on the present moment, we learn not to cling to it. All things are transient. We should enjoy them while they are here and not be distressed when they are gone. This is the essence of not stopping the mind and it is what Takuan Soho meant when he wrote, "I can only hope your mind be not detained by this transient lodging."

Life is the transient lodging and, as such, we ought not to cling to our fleeting existence. As the Indian proverb wisely warns, "Life is a bridge, pass over it but build no house upon it."

In other words, do not cling to permanence in an impermanent world. Live with what Seneca called "the eternal springboard on which mortal things rest" always in mind. Fully aware that one day we must trade this reality for one we know naught. Rather than let that thought terrify you, let it energize you, let it focus your mind, contextualize your mission, and define your path.

Transform the fear of death into fear of an unfulfilled life. Chip away at that fear with a commitment to right action and improvement over the course of a lifetime. And when the inevitability of nature does finds us, let it find us devoid of fear and regret. Our last battle is to die well. To let it all go with equanimity. To lose what we love without fear and leave a positive, lasting impact on those around us.

21
THE RIVER BECOMES THE SEA

My grandfather Goltran grew up in a small, rural town in western Cuba called San Juan Y Martínez. His father owned a small pharmacy in the center of town, and it was there that, as a young boy, Goltran first dreamed of becoming a doctor. But becoming a doctor when you live in rural Cuba and are from a family of meager means is no easy feat. Yet Goltran was not deterred.

He attended to his studies with focus and diligence despite the many challenges he faced, poverty chief among them. His family could not afford to buy him (or his sister) new clothes for school, and the other kids made fun of him for his raggedy appearance. But instead of stopping his mind there and letting the opinions of others define his narrative and limit his opportunities, he channeled his potent emotions and used them to fuel the flames of his ambition. He became the best student in his high school, eventually getting himself into medical school at the University of Havana, the best university in the country.

Things weren't any easier for him there either. He was a *guajiro* (Cuban slang for country boy) and was very much out of place in the big city. But he continued to walk his path, churning gravel underneath his feet every day with renewed conviction. Through focus, discipline, and sheer force of will, he rose to the top of his class.

Then, on March 14, 1957, when Goltran was just one semester away from completing medical school, forty-three armed students attacked the Presidential Palace with semi-automatic rifles and hand grenades, killing a palace guard as they stormed the entrance in an attempt to assassinate then dictator Fulgencio Batista. They would kill five more soldiers before being mowed down by bullets in the patio and on the stairway as they tried to reach the upper floors.

The environment for students became toxic in the wake of what came to be known as the attack on the palace (*el ataque al palacio*). Classes were suspended indefinitely, students suspected of having any kind of unsavory affiliations were rounded up wholesale, and almost everyone became radicalized in different directions.

Goltran didn't know what was coming, but he knew it wouldn't end well. Despite having worked so hard and having come so far, he knew that if he stayed it would all be for nothing. So he left, and relocated in Salamanca, Spain, where he had no family, no friends, and had to essentially start medical school over.

When Goltran did finally graduate, he decided to climb another mountain. He moved to New York City, learned English, and did his residency at an American hospital. After completing his residency, he opened a small clinic in the heart of Queens, where he would treat other immigrants, most of whom didn't speak English and rarely had money or insurance.

It was here that he met my grandmother, also a Cuban immigrant, who'd fled the Communist regime that had taken over the island since he'd left. They would eventually marry and have a son, my father. And as time went on, Goltran's small clinic became a big one. He hired additional doctors, more patients came, and things went well. But like all things in life, this momentary triumph was fleeting.

He and my grandmother grew apart and their marriage ended when my dad was still a young boy. Consequently, my grandmother and father moved to Miami where her family (who had also recently arrived from Cuba) was living. This devastated Goltran, who had come so far only to lose what he loved most. To soften the blow, he bought an apartment on Miami Beach and would come visit his son every spring and summer, for the rest of his life.

Goltran would later settle down and remarry as he continued to grow his practice. His son (my father) would go on to become a lawyer and have a son of his own, me. This made Goltran smitten, and he would visit us with even more regularity.

Some of my earliest memories are of playing on a sandy beach with him, for hours on end, during the summers of my early youth. He loved the time we spent together and wanted to increase the frequency, so he made plans to retire. Goltran planned to keep the clinic but hire additional doctors to see his patients, essentially phasing himself out of the day-to-day operations and leaving him with plenty of time to spend with his family.

But he never got to realize that dream. He was diagnosed with pancreatic cancer when he was sixty-two years old, and less than a year later, just a few months after his sixty-third birthday, he was dead. His father, the pharmacist, outlived him by five years.

Death very much caught my grandfather in the act of life. Yet he seemed indifferent to his own fate. Not in a sad way. He didn't feel sorry for himself and he wasn't angry or bitter. Instead of being resentful about his fate, it seemed like he was appreciative, as if he was thankful that he got to take the ride.

After all, he knew how fortunate he was. Most of the people he grew up with were either dead, had spent half their life in a prison cell, or, at best, were slaves to an oppressive regime, prisoners on a tropical island. Instead, my grandfather's last lodging was a two-story apartment on Park Avenue.

To him, death, like life, was just another bridge to cross, another door to pass through, and he accepted his fate unflinchingly. His cancer was already in an advanced state when the doctors found it had spread to his stomach and liver. Being a doctor himself, he knew what this meant. The likelihood of survival was slim, almost nonexistent. Treatment would require painful surgery that removed huge portions of his intestines, and, if he was lucky enough to survive that, he had chemotherapy to look forward to.

He opted not to treat his cancer. Instead he would spend his final months traveling around Spain with his son and his very last days at home surrounded by the rest of his family before quietly passing away. In a strange way, I think that losing my grandmother helped prepare him for death. He learned to lose what he loved with equanimity, as we all must, for we will all lose what we love eventually. Fear and bitterness don't lighten this load, they only make it heavier.

I don't know what happens after death, but I do know that when death comes, it will find me unafraid, as it found my grandfather, all those years ago. It is our job as warriors to die well. To be brave for the sake of those we love. Our lives are art, and death is our magnum opus, our final chapter, our last act, and we must end our saga well.

"Whether people be of high or low birth, rich or poor, old or young, enlightened or confused, they are all alike in that they will one day die. It is not that we don't know that we are going to die, but we grasp at straws. While knowing that we will die someday, we think that all the others will die before us and that we will be the last to go. Death seems a long way oft … It is indeed a capital conception. The end is important for all things. One's whole life should be like this," wrote Yamamoto Tsunetomo.

We don't look soberly at death because it scares us. Yet we must confront the frightening aspects of our reality if we wish to live a fulfilling life. It is only by confronting our fears that we can make peace with them. Through examination and contemplation, we strip things to their base and see them as they really are. Upon closer inspection all circumstances begin to lose their veneer of terror. We cannot escape the inevitability of nature, but we can escape the fear of it by simply accepting it, as my grandfather did.

Hirayama Heigen reminded that "if you are certain in your resignation to death, then fearful thoughts end, and a brave and strong heart spontaneously arises. When this brave heart is continuous, the citadel of mind is secure and you have unobstructed independent moral force."

A brave heart produces a sound mind, and a sound mind knows that death is not to be feared. Life is like a river and death is the sea. An unbounded ocean of energy from whence we came and will soon return. Our form is temporary, but our essence is eternal. The unquantifiable eternal element of existence is what Munenori called man's original mind and is our true form.

He said, "What is called the original mind is the face you had before your mother and father were born and is without form. It is not born and it does not perish."

Victory is never guaranteed, but defeat is. We will all have to deal with losses in our lifetime, and, ultimately, we will have to deal with greatest loss of all, our life. The real victory is our mindset, our mental citadel, the impenetrable fortress within.

A brave heart keeps our fortress secure from all intruders, even decay and death. We must surrender our body to the demands of nature, but not our mind. Living a full life is the best remedy for a good death. It ensures that when death does find us, it will find us free of fear and devoid of regrets, thankful for the time we were given and proud of what we did with it.

By all accounts Takuan Soho lived an extraordinary life. Revered for his wisdom, he was council to Daimyos, friend and mentor to legendary warriors, and was even given his own temple and estate to govern as he saw fit. But when his end did come, he met it with the same indifference the warriors he counseled met theirs. He instructed his followers to "bury my body in the mountain behind the temple, cover it in dirt, and go home. Read no sutras, and hold no ceremony. Receive no gifts from either monk or laity. Let the monks wear their robes, eat their meals, and carry on as normal days."

We train our whole life, fortify our mind, and feed our souls, and when the end does come, we feed the earth with our flesh, in much the same way that it nourished us. All things are cyclical, an eternal game of give and take of which we are lucky to have been a part. We should not be bitter that our time is at an end but, like my grandfather, happy that we got to take the ride.

The mind that does not stop with things will not be stained by them, even death. Let us meet our end unmarred by fear and regret, as Takuan Soho met his. And as we are propelled downstream by the tide of our life, wherever it may take us, let us remember that every river becomes the sea eventually.

AFTERWORD

Yagyū Munenori reminded us that "learning is the gate that approaches the Way. Passing through this gate you arrive at the Way. But learning is only the gate … Do not read written works and think this is the Way."

Now you must pass through the gate and put these principles into practice in your own life. As you travel your path, however, you will undoubtedly encounter obstacles, detours, and distractions.

Written works may not be the Way, but they can serve as guiding markers. A way to illuminate your path and stay on course when darkness inevitably falls. The more you familiarize yourself with these texts, the clearer your path becomes. Books will not take action for you, but they will help you decide which actions to take.

I regularly reread the works cited in the next sections and find that each time I do, it's a refreshing and cleansing experience that realigns my internal compass and allows me to continue on my journey with renewed focus and conviction.

The masters who wrote these works were not armchair philosophers. They were, for the most part, warriors, and their writing was meant to sustain a soul under the harshest of conditions. To give it the power to flower and flourish not in spite of, but rather because of, those dire circumstances.

But you've merely scratched the surface. To actuate these principles in your own life, you must immerse yourself in their wisdom and renew your focus regularly, both in good times and in bad. I recognize how difficult this can be, especially in the face of the overwhelming responsibilities that life places on us. Yet this is the nature of the Way. It is a difficult, lifelong commitment that most people will never realize.

But you are not most people. You are a warrior, and if you face your demons with open eyes and an empty mind, your inner citadel will never fall. Meet your enemy on the field then, offer them no quarter, and seek no retreat. The weakness in your soul that once reigned supreme is gone, dead, slayed. Replaced by a steady heart and sound mind that fears nothing between life and death.

When darkness does fall, fortify your mind with the words of the masters. Do not let their lessons wash over you, but rather absorb them and return to them, time and time again, remembering always that the pursuit of excellence is a lifelong commitment that is ended only by death.

The books listed in the next sections were instrumental tools that helped me find my path and continue to sustain me as I travel it. They are both old and new texts, but their wisdom is timeless. Though the route may differ, they all point to the same destination.

READING FOR WARRIORS

The Life-Giving Sword: Secret Teachings from the House of the Shogun by Yagyū Munenori (Translated by William Scott Wilson)

Yagyū Munenori was a lowly born samurai who would rise to become a Daimyo. His seminal work, *The Life-Giving Sword*, was meant to be an instructional manual for the warriors he commanded. Given its context, one would expect *The Life-Giving Sword* to be a dry text rooted in practicality. Yet it contains far more than just pure military strategy. Munenori spends almost the entire text analyzing and articulating the mindset that leads to excellence and fortifies the soul. He says it is with this mindset and this mindset alone that a warrior can hope to achieve greatness. Munenori believes that this mindset can be applied to every domain of life, and it is only when we have achieved this mindset in all of our affairs that we are truly free. In *The Life-Giving Sword* Munenori draws us a map to that freedom.

The Unfettered Mind: Writings from a Zen Master to a Master Swordsman by Takuan Soho (Translated by William Scott Wilson)

Mostly philosophical in nature and grounded heavily in Buddhist teachings, *The Unfettered Mind* frames combat as a vehicle for self-transcendence. Soho found refuge from the volatility of his time in Buddhism. Even though warfare is the primary subject matter of his writing, an aura of tranquility permeates the text. Takuan was not only influential in his lifetime, his teachings would be revered by generations of samurai long after his death, his ideas validated by men who knocked on death's door with indifference. What better endorsement can we ask for?

The Book of Five Rings by Miyamoto Musashi (Translated by William Scott Wilson)

The book is mostly an instructional manual for combat, but strewn throughout it are philosophical gems that give us an insight into Musashi's mindset. A mindset that elevated him from mere mortal to legend. Musashi was an undefeated wandering warrior who adhered to no rules but his own. First fighting with two swords and then, at the end of his long martial career, none at all. Yes, you read that right. He would face fierce warriors unarmed and, in the heat of combat, take and strike them down with their own sword. To many observers this must have seemed like madness. But, in truth, Musashi's ability came from a constant refinement of the principles of combat that he honed over the course of a lifetime. In *The Book of Five Rings* we delve into that insight and gain a better understand of the mindset that drove his legendary achievements.

Hagakure: The Secret Wisdom of the Samurai by Yamamoto Tsunetomo (Translated by Alexander Bennett)

Yamamoto Tsunetomo created a moral manual for his retainers that was meant to guide their conduct. Concerned with what he perceived to be the decaying morals of his time, he decided to preserve the pillars of the warrior's way in writing. Though much of the text is concerned with customs and proper samurai etiquette, a significant portion of the writing deals with manifesting the warrior's spirt.

Training the Samurai Mind: A Bushido Sourcebook by Thomas Cleary

In *Training the Samurai Mind*, Cleary translates a collection of texts written by samurai in different eras that gives us an insight into their enduring principles.

Great by Choice: Uncertainty, Chaos, and Luck--Why Some Thrive Despite Them All by Jim Collins and Morten T. Hansen

On the surface, *Great by Choice* is a book about business that has nothing to do with the way of the warrior. However, the strategies that work on a macro level to make institutions great also work on a micro level and can make individuals great. By learning to how to empirically validate our decisions and create regimented outputs as a result of that validation, we are given a framework with which we can surmount the seemingly insurmountable obstacles that prevent us from reaching our full potential and fulfilling our true purpose.

The Black Swan: The Impact of the Highly Improbable by Nassim Nicholas Taleb

Uncertainty is the only certainty. Fortifying the inner citadel so that we may thrive in uncertain and chaotic conditions is what the samurai mindset is all about. Taleb is the master of thriving in uncertainty. A financier turned philosopher who firmly understands the limits of human knowledge and the limitlessness of human hubris, Taleb has made a fortune betting on both. As warriors we seek to observe events from an elevated vantage point so that we may glimpse their inner workings, to see with what Musashi called the perceiving eye. Taleb helps us hone that vision.

Turning Pro: Tap Your Inner Power and Create Your Life's Work by Steven Pressfield

You wouldn't be reading this book if it weren't for Steven Pressfield. When you read *Turning Pro* you will be set on a collision course with whichever mountain you secretly wish to climb. I listened to *Turning Pro* over and over again as I walked to jujitsu for months on end, during the production of this book. That repetition cemented my path, narrowed my focus, and kept me dedicated to the completion of this book. Whatever unfulfilled ambition brought you here, Pressfield will turn that ember of passion into a raging fire that can no longer be ignored.

Letters from a Stoic by Lucius Annaeus Seneca (Translated by Richard Gummere)

Seneca is one of my favorite writers. Like many samurai, he was born in an era of violence and uncertainty. The principles Seneca espouses in his writing bear an uncanny similarity to the philosophy that guided the samurai. Stoicism, the school of philosophy to which Seneca belonged, is in alignment with the warrior's way and can help guide us on our path. Of all the Stoic writers, I find Seneca to be the most accessible and the most enjoyable.

High Performance Habits: How Extraordinary People Become That Way by Brendon Burchard

High Performance Habits is the best book I've ever read for personal development, period. It gives the reader tangible methods to actuate potential that are corroborated by data. In this book I've tried to point you in the right direction. Burchard gives you the tools to go from observation to action.

Get Three Free eBooks

Building a relationship with readers is one of the best parts of my job. As a thank-you for your time and attention. I'd like to send you a free eBook every month for the next three months.

What are the books about? Samurai, of course. Every month I'll send you a quick-read, in digital format, about the life and legacy of a legendary samurai warrior. You'll read about their exploits and explore the enduring principles that define their legacy.

In addition to free monthly books, I'm part of an author's group that has some talented writers in it, and occasionally they give their books away to select readers. In addition to my writing, you will automatically receive invites to these book giveaways when you join the community.

If you want to get free eBooks,
visit <u>SamuraiReader.com</u>
and tell me where to send them.

Did you enjoy this book?
You can make a huge difference!

I need your help. Reviews are the single most powerful tool in my arsenal to get visibility for my books. As much as I'd like to, I don't have the financial muscle of a large corporate publisher. But I have something else, something entrenched publishers envy: A legion of likeminded warriors, and together we can spread the light.

If you enjoyed this book and think its message is worth sharing, please help get the word out by spending a few minutes and leaving a review on Amazon. It can be as short as you like.

BIBLIOGRAPHY

Adler, Jerry. "Why Fire Makes Us Human." *Smithsonian Magazine*, June 2013.

Clearly, Thomas. *Training the Samurai Mind: A Bushido Sourcebook.* Boston, London: Shambhala, 2011. Contains writing from, Shōsan Suzuki, Kaneyoshi Ichijo, Yoshimasa Shiba, Heigen Hirayama, Masahiro Adachi, and Soko Yamaga

Collins, Jim and Morten T. Hansen. *Great by Choice: Uncertainty, Chaos and Luck—Why Some Thrive Despite Them All.* New York: Harper Collins, 2011.

Doerr, John. *Measure What Matters: How Google, Bono, and the Gates Foundation Rock the World with OKRs.* New York: Portfolio / Penguin, 2018.

Ferrazzi, Keith and Tahl Raz. *Never Eat Alone: And Other Secrets to Success, One Relationship at a Time.* New York: Crown Business, 2005.

Maslin, Mark. "Why Did Humans Evolve Such Large Brains? Because Smarter People Have More Friends." *The Conversation*, June 2017.

Munenori, Yagyū. *The Life-Giving Sword: Secret Teachings from the House of the Shogun.* Translated by William Scott Wilson. Boston: Shambhala Publications, 2012.

Muneyoshi, Naganuma. *Training the Samurai Mind: A Bushido Sourcebook.* Translated and edited by Thomas Cleary. Boston: Shambhala Publications, 2011.

Musashi, Miyamoto. *The Book of Five Rings.* Translated by William Scott Wilson. Boston: Shambhala Publications, 2012.

Pirsig, Robert M. *Zen and the Art of Motorcycle Maintenance: An Inquiry into Values.*

New York: William Morrow, 1974.

Pressfield, Steven. *Turning Pro: Tap Your Inner Power and Create Your Life's Work.*

New York: Black Irish Entertainment, 2012.

Seneca, Lucius Annaeus. *Letters from a Stoic.* Translated by Richard Gummere. Edited by Chandran Prasa. Lexicos Publishing, 2011.

Soho, Takuan. *The Unfettered Mind: Writings from a Zen Master to a Master Swordsman.* Translated by William Scott Wilson. Boston: Shambhala Publications, 2012.

Stout, Dietrich and Thierry Chaminade. "Stone Tools, Language, and the Brain in Human Evolution." Philosophical Transactions of the Royal Society B: Biological Sciences 367, no. 1585 (January 2012): 75–87.

Taleb, Nassim Nicholas. *The Black Swan: The Impact of the Highly Improbable.* New York: Random House, 2007.

Tsunetomo, Yamamoto. *Hagakure: The Secret Wisdom of the Samurai.* Translated by Alexander Bennett. Tokyo: Tuttle Publishing, 2014.

ABOUT THE AUTHOR

Ryan Perez is a writer, serial entrepreneur, and Brazilian Jujitsu competitor. Originally from Miami, he currently lives and works in Medellin, Colombia.

Prior to becoming an author, Ryan was the Chief Marketing Officer of a company that he cofounded (Urban Drones), a tech start-up that manufactured the first waterproof consumer drone on the market. He then cofounded Lepton, a niche marketing company that has helped top tech start-ups acquire millions of users.

Far from always having been an achiever, Ryan struggled with mediocrity all his life until he developed a passion for and began competing in Brazilian Jujitsu. He would use the principles he learned on the mat to overcome his fears, transform his character, and create his writing career. Because of the positive impact jujitsu had on Ryan's life, he is now an evangelist for the martial arts lifestyle.

Killing Weakness is Ryan's first book. When he's not writing, reading, or training, Ryan enjoys hiking and watching streaming series with his dog, Cain, an Italian mastiff. You can connect with Ryan directly on Telegram (@RyanPerez), on Instagram (r_pk3), or via email at Ryan@lepton.io

CPSIA information can be obtained
at www.ICGtesting.com
Printed in the USA
BVHW022336220322
632091BV00019B/1370